Anna Karenina

The Bitterness of Ecstasy

TWAYNE'S MASTERWORK STUDIES

Robert Lecker, General Editor

———————————————

Anna Karenina

The Bitterness of Ecstasy

Gary Adelman

Twayne Publishers • Boston
A *Division of* G. K. Hall & Co.

Anna Karenina: The Bitterness of Ecstasy
Gary Adelman

Copyright 1990 by G. K. Hall & Co.
All rights reserved.
Published by Twayne Publishers
A division of G. K. Hall & Co.
70 Lincoln Street
Boston, Massachusetts 02111

Copyediting supervised by Barbara Sutton
Book production by Gabrielle B. McDonald
Typeset in 10/14 Sabon with ITC Novarese Medium display type
by Compositors Corporation, Cedar Rapids, Iowa

Printed and bound in the United States of America.

Library of Congress Cataloging-in-Publication Data

Adelman, Gary.
    Anna Karenina : the bitterness of ecstasy / Gary Adelman.
       p.   cm. — (Twayne's masterwork studies ; no. 56)
    Includes bibliographical references.
       1. Tolstoy, Leo, graf, 1828–1910. Anna Karenina.   I. Title.
    II. Series.
    PG3365.A63A34   1990
    891.73'3—dc20   90-4314
                                                                 CIP

0.8057.8083.1 (alk. paper) 10 9 8 7 6 5 4 3 2 1
0.8057.8139.0 (pbk. alk. paper) 10 9 8 7 6 5 4 3 2 1
First published 1990.

... nequiquam, quoniam medio de fonte leporum
surgit amari aliquid quod in ipsis floribus angat ...

... in vain: for from the midst of the fountain of delights
something bitter arises to choke them among the very flowers ...
—Lucretius, *De Rerum Natura* 4.1133–34

Contents

Contents

Note on the References
and Acknowledgments

All page references to *Anna Karenina* are to the Modern Library College Edition, translated by Constance Garnett and edited and introduced by Leonard J. Kent and Nina Berberova (New York: Modern Library, 1965). The first number cited parenthetically in the text refers to the part, followed by a colon and chapter number of the citation.

I would like to take this opportunity to thank the University of Illinois Research Board and Judith Liebman for supporting this work and making available to me the invaluable assistance of Michael Armstrong and Norma Marder—who together edited the manuscript—and of Elsie Pettit. I am particularly indebted to Norma for the overall clarity and finish of the work.

I am also grateful to Herbert Marder and Edward Wasiolek for taking the time to read the manuscript and offer marginal comments, and especially to Gary Jahn, whose lengthy, detailed critique of my work was a real boon.

The office staff of the University of Illinois English Department—and especially Carol Pagliara and Anne Moore—kindly assisted me. The frontispiece was designed for this book by Carlton Bruett.

Finally, I wish to thank my wife, Phyllis Rider Adelman, for finding time to proofread the manuscript and make final refinements.

Designed by Carlton Bruett.

Chronology: Leo Tolstoy's Life and Works

1828	Leo Nikolaevich Tolstoy born 9 September (28 August, Old Style), youngest of four brothers, at the family estate, Yasnaya Polyana, south of Moscow. His father, Count Nikolai Ilych Tolstoy, had served in the Russian army in the campaign of 1812; captured by the French the following year, he had been released when Paris fell in 1814.
1830	Mother, Maria Nikolaevna, née Bolkonskaya, dies 4 August.
ca. 1834	His brother Nikolay assures him that on a green stick buried at the edge of a ravine in a nearby forest are carved words "that would destroy all the evil in the hearts of men and bring them everything good." At his own request, Leo Tolstoy was to be buried on this spot.
1837	Family moves to Moscow; father dies 20 June.
1844	Studies Oriental languages at the University of Kazan; fails end-of-year examinations and transfers to the faculty of law.
1847	Treated for venereal disease. Inherits Yasnaya Polyana and leaves the university to devote himself to the estate and to the welfare of his serfs.
1848	Moves to Moscow and plunges into fashionable life and debauchery.
1851	Leaves for the Caucasus with brother Nikolay; takes part as volunteer in military campaigns.
1852	*Childhood* greeted with favorable reviews. Joins army as a "junker" (a person not subject to military discipline, but allowed to share quarters with regular officers and to participate in maneuvers and operations).
1854	*Boyhood.* Receives army commission; is transferred to the Danube.
1855	Czar Nicholas I dies; Alexander II accedes to throne. Tolstoy serves at the siege of Sevastopol. *The Memoirs of a Billiard*

Marker, Sevastopol in December, Sevastopol in May, The Woodfelling. Notes in his diary, 4 March: "the founding of a new religion appropriate to the stage of development of mankind—the religion of Christ, but purged of beliefs and mysticism, a practical religion, not promising future bliss but giving bliss on earth." After fall of Sevastopol, frequents St. Petersburg literary circles, meeting Goncharov, Turgenev, and others.

1856   *Sevastopol in August, The Snowstorm, Two Hussars, A Landowner's Morning.* Retires from army; active in social circles of St. Petersburg.

1857   *Youth* and *Lucerne.* Travels in Western Europe (January–July). Shocked at witnessing a public execution in Paris.

1858   *Albert.* Nearly killed by a bear while hunting.

1859   *Three Deaths* and *Family Happiness.* Starts school for peasant children at Yasnaya Polyana: "I think I've given up literature for good."

1860   Travels in Italy and England; visits schools in Germany and France; unimpressed. Horrified at watching the death (by consumption) of his brother Nikolay: "When one really comes to think that death is the end of everything, then there is nothing worse than being alive. . . . Nikolenka's death has hit me harder than anything I have ever experienced."

1861   Emancipation of the serfs 19 February. Tolstoy returns to Russia and to literature. Resumes teaching. Quarrels with Turgenev and challenges him to a duel; both eventually apologize but do not speak or write to each other for the next seventeen years.

1862   Produces educational journal *Yasnaya Polyana.* Police raid his home 6–7 July to search his papers, diaries, and correspondence. Marries Sofia Andreyevna Behrs 23 September. Closes school.

1863   *The Cossacks* and *Polikushka.* First child born. Begins work on *War and Peace.*

1865   Publishes *1805* (first part of *War and Peace*).

1869   Publishes sixth (final) volume of *War and Peace.* Studies Schopenhauer. In a hotel room at Arzamas on 2 September experiences panic and terror of death: "My whole being ached with the need to live, the right to live, and, at the same moment, I felt death at work. And it was awful, being torn apart inside. . . . [T]here is nothing in life, nothing exists but death, and death should not be!"

1870   Studies Greek intensively. First mention of *Anna Karenina* recorded in his wife's diary 23 February: "Yesterday evening he told me he had envisaged a certain type of woman, married, of high society, who had gone astray. He said his object was to make this woman merely pitiable, and not guilty."

1871	Recuperates during summer from an illness by traveling to the South Urals and drinking *kumys*—fermented mare's milk. Begins writing a new pedagogical work, the *Primer*.
1872	*Primer: A Prisoner in the Caucasus, God Sees the Truth but Waits*. Researches a novel about Peter the Great. Reopens Yasnaya Polyana school.
1873	Begins writing *Anna Karenina* 18 March.
1874	Writes and lectures on pedagogy. Bored with *Anna Karenina*: "I want to give it up, I dislike it so much."
1875	*New Primer* and *Russian Reader*. First sections of *Anna Karenina* published in the *Russian Messenger*. 16 February: "It can't be, and it oughtn't to be a great success, particularly the first chapters which are decidedly weak. I can see that, and it hurts me." 9 November: "My God, if only someone would finish *A. Karenina* for me! It's unbearably repulsive."
1876	Further sections of *Anna Karenina* published.
1877	Deeply disturbed about Russo-Turkish War. The *Russian Messenger* refuses to print the eighth and final part of *Anna Karenina* without substantial cuts because of its ridicule of Russian military participation in the war. Tolstoy publishes part 8 separately. Increasingly absorbed in religion; prays daily, attends Mass, observes fasts.
1878	*Anna Karenina* published in book form. Reconciliation with Turgenev. Works on a novel about the Decembrist uprising of 1825. His religious crisis is at its height.
1879	Continues work on the Decembrist novel. Visits several monasteries and begins to write *Confession*.
1880	More work on *Confession*. Begins *A Criticism of Dogmatic Theology* and *A Translation and Harmony of the Four Gospels*.
1881	A terrorist's bomb kills Czar Alexander II; he is succeeded by his son Alexander III. Tolstoy writes to the new czar urging him (in vain) not to hang the assassins. *What Men Live By*.
1882	Working as a census-taker in Moscow, he is horrified by conditions in the slums. Finishes *Confession*; it is banned as heretical. Studies Hebrew and the Old Testament.
1883	Turgenev writes from his deathbed, "My friend, return to literature!" First meeting with Vladimir Grigor'evich Chertkov, a

young officer who will later become Tolstoy's chief "disciple," the foremost of the "Tolstoyans" and Sofia's hated enemy.

1884   Finishes *What I Believe*; police raid the printer and confiscate all copies. Studies Oriental religions and cobbling. Frequent quarrels with his wife: "Until the day I die she will be a stone around my neck and the necks of my children. I must learn not to drown with this stone around my neck."

1885   Attempts to give up hunting, meat, alcohol, tobacco, and white bread. Increasing friction with his family.

1886   *The Death of Ivan Ilych.* During the summer, agricultural labor with peasants.

1887   *The Power of Darkness.* Performance and sale of copies of the drama banned by order of the czar: "This ignominious L. Tolstoy must be stopped. He is nothing but a nihilist and non-believer." The play was, however, later permitted and in the mid-1890s became one of the great successes of Stanislavsky's and Nemirovich-Danchenko's Moscow Art Theatre.

1888   Thirteenth (and last) child born. Continuing family troubles.

1889   Writes *The Kreutzer Sonata*, which advocates chastity, even in marriage.

1890   *The Kreutzer Sonata* banned. During a personal audience with the czar, his wife secures permission for the story to be published in the *Collected Works.*

1891   Renounces copyright to his works published since 1881; gives his property to his family. Organizes relief for famine in Ryazan Province.

1893   Writes *The Kingdom of God Is within You*; sends it abroad for publication. In Moscow, depressed by "this luxury. This sale of books. This moral filth. This fuss and bother.... The main thing is I want to suffer, I want to shout out the truth which is burning me."

1895   *Master and Man.*

1896   Begins writing *Hadji Murat* (published posthumously).

1898   *What Is Art?* published in a censored version.

1899   *Resurrection.*

1901   Excommunicated by the Orthodox church; cheered by crowds in Moscow. Publishes *Reply to the Synod's Edict.* A journalist writes, "We have two czars, Nicholas II and Leo Tolstoy.... Let anyone lift a finger against Tolstoy and the whole world will be up in arms and our administration will turn tail and run!"

1902	Writes to the czar to urge him to abolish private ownership of land.
1903	Protests against Jewish pogroms; contributes three stories to an anthology in aid of pogrom victims.
1904	*Bethink Yourselves!* published, a tract against the Russo-Japanese War.
1905	Writes *Alyosha Gorshok* and other stories.
1906	Quashes efforts to award him the Nobel Prize for literature.
1908	*I Cannot Be Silent* (against capital punishment of revolutionaries). The article is banned; editors who print excerpts are fined or arrested. Tolstoy records the article, in Russian, French, and English, on a dictating machine sent him by Thomas Edison.
1909	Frequent quarrels with his wife; at one point she threatens suicide. 12 July: "If only she knew and understood how she alone is poisoning the last hours, days, months of my life! But I can't say so, and I don't expect any words to have any effect on her."
1910	Corresponds with Mahatma Gandhi on the doctrine of nonresistance to evil. Awakening at 3 A.M. on 28 October, hears his wife rummaging through his papers and decides to leave home for good. When Sofia learns of his flight, she attempts suicide. Ill with pneumonia, he arrives by train at the Astapovo station 31 October. A priest comes 6 November in hopes of bringing him back to the Orthodox church; the doctors do not permit him to approach the patient. Dies 7 November and is buried two days later at Yasnaya Polyana, at the ravine where the "green stick" bearing the secret of happiness had supposedly been hidden.

Situating the Text

1

Historical Context

The reign of Alexander II, the czar-emancipator, 1855 to 1881, was the golden age of the Russian novel. This is the period of the great works of Turgenev, Dostoyevsky, and Tolstoy, works that constitute Russia's principal contribution to European literature. One must look to the decades of English literary history between 1590 and 1610, the time of Spenser, Marlowe, Donne, Jonson, and Shakespeare, to find another such efflorescence.

Alexander became emperor on 19 February 1855, during the debacle of the Crimean War. The fall of Sevastopol several months after his coronation, and the negotiated peace with England and France at the Treaty of Paris, marked a low point in Russia's international position. Russia, at the time of the Crimean War, was a poor agrarian society. Industry was barely developed. Agricultural techniques were backward, and serfdom was the basic social institution. The war demonstrated that Russia had fallen behind the rapidly industrializing nations of Europe and that social changes had to be instituted if it were to compete effectively. Therefore Alexander was conciliatory to demands for fundamental changes in government and society. Moreover, the disastrous war raised the specter of a massive peasant rebellion. The caprices of history put this eldest son of the Germanophile autocrat, Nicholas I, in the position of presiding over a series of liberal reforms that, while not revolutionary, fostered the emergence of a revolutionary movement, a faction of which assassinated him in 1881.

Alexander disbanded his father's secret police, eased restraints on censorship, and permitted more open and diverse expressions of opinion. Literary journals came into prominence, the number growing from about 15 to 110 during his reign. They divided into factions and engaged in ideological wars. The radical camp promoted utilitarian art totally dedicated to serving the cause of social progress. It rejected any kind of appeal to Christian moral values, proclaiming science and rationality as entirely sufficient to solve social problems. The reactionary camp (the patriotic Slavophile journals) rejected European enlightenment, and sought to preserve the traditions and morality of Russia's past. It promoted literary works that celebrated the positive, moral values to be found in the nobility and the peasantry. The liberal gentry, prowestern and progressive, held the middle ground. In general, the intelligentsia, especially the new generation, was allied with the radical camp. The intellectual ferment released by the easing of restraints turned into unrest in the months just after the emancipation of the serfs, when St. Petersburg was deluged by seditious leaflets. The government suppressed the leading radical journal, deporting its editor to Siberia, and demanded political orthodoxy from all the journals; yet, despite these constraints, social and political issues dominated the journals, swallowing up purely artistic concerns. Literature was discussed as ideology—evaluated for what it said about the interest of the peasants, the rights of women, the responsibility of the intelligentsia, the mission of Russia, and the future destiny of mankind. Tolstoy published most of *War and Peace*, as well as *Anna Karenina*, in the *Russian Messenger*, a patriotic journal that admired everything Russian and resisted everything European.

The freedom of public expression and the emergence of a new class, the intelligentsia—largely opposed to the patriarchal rights of the landed gentry—helped Alexander to abolish serfdom by decree on 19 February 1861. Under the new law, the government issued bonds to the nobles that paid for the peasants' freedom and a portion of the land they had worked. The peasants, then, repaid the government over a forty-nine-year period, the bonds serving to compensate the nobles for the fair value of the lost land and for the lost labor as well. The government attempted to prevent the development of a class of landless peasants by making each village responsible for all its families, hoping that collective responsibility would strengthen the peasant village as a social unit and thus minimize the danger of massive unrest. Through his hero and surrogate, Levin, Tolstoy portrays the landed gentry's dilemma in *Anna Karenina*, sympathizing with Levin's struggles to deal with land reform in a way that sustains both Levin's moral sense and his privileges. The emancipation dealt a mortal blow to the gentry, and many of its ruined members were absorbed into the intelligentsia.

Alexander radically reformed the judiciary to provide for the new legal status of the peasants as free men, adopting many Western principles—equality before the law, equal access to the law, due process, trial by jury—and transforming the judiciary from one of the worst to one of the best in the civilized world. He established zemtzvos, or elected administrative bodies that supervised education, public health, and the upkeep of roads, local functions that formerly had been under the control of the imperial bureaucracy. The establishment of these elected assemblies marked a significant step toward popular participation, and Russian liberals hoped that it would soon lead to a national parliament. They were disappointed.

Levin's contempt for the zemtzvos in *Anna Karenina* represents Tolstoy's general opposition toward efforts at modernizing Russia. As he saw it, modernization destroyed the values of rural life as well as the land itself; with material progress came spiritual destruction. The railroad, in particular, symbolized the evil that came from the West. For agricultural Russia to export grain and industrialize, railway lines were needed. Alexander was a passionate builder of railroads. At the time of the Crimean War, there were less than 800 miles of railroad track in the whole country; when Tolstoy began writing *Anna Karenina*, there were over 14,000 miles of track. By the end of the 1870s, a class of modern factory workers was living in suburbs outside Moscow and St. Petersburg. But it was precisely this centralization of industry in towns—this artificial engrafting of civilization from without, and the decadence that arises from the increase of leisure—that Tolstoy blamed for the impoverishment of Russia.

Tolstoy belonged by birth to the upper stratum of the ruling class. He always remained a class-conscious nobleman and kept aloof from the intelligentsia, regarding its members as entirely artificial, useless, and untrustworthy creatures who knew nothing of war or farming—who were nourished on books, not on life—and yet who claimed the right to instruct their fellows. He believed in being as un-European as possible and had no use for bourgeois aspirations. Alexander's reforms created debates between the classes into which Tolstoy threw himself with energy. The major debate concerned the system of farming that was to be adopted by the new mass of emancipated workers. Tolstoy regarded the problem from the perspective of a country squire—one of, as Levin exclaims proudly, the *real* aristocrats who stick to the land and the old paternal order as if "we were ancient vestals set to keep some sacred fire going" (6:29). Tolstoy's chief adversaries were the proponents of revolutionary socialism and the liberal wing of the land-holding gentry that advocated European advances in agricultural technology and economy and the education of the peasantry as solutions to Russia's agrarian problems. He was persuaded that Russia's problems had nothing to do with the anomalous distribution of property and that the strength of Russia, its backbone, was the paternal gentry, whose way of life would be destroyed by capitalism and an educated peasantry. He believed that Western theories were nonsensical and dangerous and that socialism could be defeated by working to preserve the peasant's traditions and values.

One sees Tolstoy between 1859 and 1862 arduously preoccupied with teaching peasant children and publicizing his school and his pedagogical theories in an educational magazine he printed at his own expense. Again, between 1870 and 1875 he devoted immense labor to compiling material for a complete course in elementary education. Behind these educational activities was a passionate conviction that the intelligentsia should learn from the peasants, since peasants had a wisdom unknown to intellectuals. From one perspective, Tolstoy's theory of education "is based on a point of view that is identical with that of Rousseau. His originality consists mainly in applying Rousseau's ideas to Russian conditions; in carrying out in actual experience with a school of peasant children ideas that Rousseau had enunciated with very little regard to working conditions" (Noyes 1918, 121–22). From another perspective, Tolstoy consistently denied that the Russian peasant could or should engage in the struggle to raise himself from the mud, and his experimental school was aimed at preventing the development of a class of landless peasants. His school was a kind of family in which the teacher acted as parent, in which lessons were informal chats, in which there was no learning by rote and rigor of discipline, and in which little was learned in the conventional sense. During the writing of *Anna Karenina*, he was supervising no fewer than seventy schools and planning a seminary for the training of peasant teachers. Yet independent schools such as the one he established at Yasnaya Polyana were forbidden, and the authorities regarded him as politically unreliable.

Although Tolstoy belonged, if anywhere, to the reactionary camp, he was irreverent toward all the conventions of state and society. He was a military man and served in the Caucasus, yet came to deride the military and sought to abolish the whole governmental order it supported. He despised the literary coteries that esteemed him and eventually rejected his own literary masterpieces. During a prolonged and active bachelorhood he fantasized about family life, and when he married found that marriage was a hindrance. He had no close friends and spoiled the few relationships he had with fellow writers. Many of his biographers describe him as an egomaniac. All discern in him, from the very beginning, an obstinate search for a rational meaning to life, a search that was reaching the proportions of a histrionic midlife religious conversion at the time of *Anna Karenina*, and which is memorably recorded both in the novel and in his *Confession*, which follows it. He emerged from this crisis a political anarchist, intensely immersed in theological matters and tortured by his attempts to reshape himself, his family, and the world.

In a letter discovered years after his death, Tolstoy describes how Pushkin's *Tales of Belkin*, particularly the fragment beginning, "the guests were arriving at the country house," sparked the process of writing *Anna*

Karenina, a process that turned out to be tortuous. *Anna Karenina* is a spiritual autobiography. Its subject, in a real sense, is Tolstoy himself, and the writing is an attempt to manage the dramas and inner conflicts of his personal life. Through Levin, he searches for a meaning to life that is both rational and capable of assuaging his obsessive fear of death. In the period during which the novel was written, two of Tolstoy's children died and Sophia had a miscarriage. Death, always on his mind, is personified by Levin's brother, the all-too-intimate Nikolai, whose lingering, ghastly death pushes Levin to make the leap of faith. But in order to believe in the consolations of faith, Tolstoy had to renounce a longing to be vulgarly alive and passionate. There is, in fact, as much of Tolstoy in the figure of Anna as in Levin. Aspects of his passionate nature also provide material for the unrepentant bon vivant, Stiva Oblonsky, Anna's brother, a man Levin loves despite himself. In the course of the novel, Tolstoy tried to find an acceptable resolution to the split in himself represented by Levin and Anna—a resolution, that is, to the terrible dilemma of being born into an earthly paradise and having to grow old and die. Most profoundly, Tolstoy himself, homo duplex, is the subject of his novel.

2

The Importance of the Work

The two lives contrasted in *Anna Karenina*'s contrapuntal design represent answers to the riddle of existence in a world ostensibly without transcendent meaning. Tolstoy intends to reveal the good life and warn against self-indulgence, but one of the virtues of the work as a whole is that it is far too ambiguous to be read in this way. Anna simply steals the show; she is too vital and mysterious to be typed as a warning, and thus she escapes or rather transcends Tolstoy's condemnation. In physical description of character Tolstoy has never been surpassed, and in Anna he creates a heroine who has intrigued generations of readers. We cannot claim to know her—why she married a frigid bureaucrat twenty years her senior, why she refuses his generous offer of a divorce, and why she disintegrates from a beautiful and life-loving woman to a destructive harpy. The novel is a stupendous study of guilty passion, and we continue to love and even admire Anna to the bitter end.

"My heart in hiding / Stirred for a bird," says Hopkins in "The Windhover," describing a magnificent falcon in flight, a symbol of the passionate self that must be repudiated in order to live a life worthy in the eyes of God. Through the novel's form, Tolstoy attempts to repudiate Anna, counterpointing the tragedy of her life with that of his hero and surrogate, Levin. Levin's problem, put simply, is how to feel zest for life in the face of death. Nineteenth-century skepticism has shaken the foundations of his being. Evolutionary process, with its rule of impersonal law, has taken the place of Creation; the earth has become "a speck of mildew" in an infinite nothingness. Through faith, Levin finds freedom from the torments and vanities of consciousness, the only kind of freedom that, to Tolstoy, is not pathological and obscene.

The voice of the narration and the comprehensiveness of its vision are remarkable and work in behalf of ambiguity rather than moral clarity. Indeed, the truth implicit in the sensuousness and tragic grandeur of the novel is distinctly antagonistic to the moral scheme enacted by the double plot. To paraphrase D. H. Lawrence, Tolstoy, like Sophocles and Shakespeare, creates a great background, vital and vivid, which matters more than the people who move upon it, and the effect of setting the pathetic pattern of man's moral life against the enormity of nature is to include Anna in that enormity, celebrating her spirit and passion as she breaks with convention into something wildly personal. The effect of the whole is of a monumental grandeur, a stateliness, an ornateness of pomp. It is a world looked upon by a godlike intelligence who sees everything in perspective, having full knowledge of truth and of the deceptions to which humankind is prone. The intelligence looks into the intimate self of his creations with the same clear, distanced gaze as at the spectacle of a horse race, portraying tragic suffering with a disinterestedness that seems almost pitiless. Tolstoy's vision has about it an astringency, a toughness and honesty about the nature of reality, that is refreshing and salutary.

One of the virtues of *Anna Karenina* is that it elicits so many diverse interpretations. It has been read as a tragedy of social oppression and failed liberation, with the emphasis on Tolstoy as a celebrator of sensuous life and sexual love. It has been read as a religious allegory, the work of a theologian belonging to a tradition of eastern Christian thought that teaches that life is a mission of loving service. It has been read as the work of a violent antihumanist whose antagonism to nineteenth-century thought and all things European looks toward the barbarism of Stalin and Hitler. The novel is celebrated for its fidelity to history with Tolstoy as the poet of the post-emancipation era, whose mirror on agrarian problems and the rise of capitalism forecasts the coming of the Russian Revolution. It has been read as a psychodrama in which Tolstoy reveals, by means of parallel story lines, his fear of supplanting the idealized image of his mother and his distorted attitude toward sexual love.

Tolstoy, despite himself, is incapable of being doctrinaire. His gaze is fixed on life and earth rather than on God and abnormality. Unlike Dostoyevsky, he doesn't create a poetry of neurosis—he is too lucid. He shuns metaphysical systems. He is too sensuous, too much the epic poet, to limit life to a representation of ideas. One of his most recent biographers says that in writing *Anna Karenina*, Tolstoy attempts "an artistic suicide every bit as final as Anna's actual suicide on the railroad" (Wilson 1988, 267). It is possible to read *Anna Karenina* as Tolstoy's swan song, as the final achievement of a great writer who, as he ceases to be interested in writing novels, emerges as a Christian thinker on the verge of creating a whole new body of work. Yet novelists, finding themselves inescapably looking to Tolstoy's example, are struck by the same thing— the amazing illusion of life, so vividly distinct and comprehensive— whether it is a swarm of gnats, or the devastating clarity of Levin and Anna's interior lives. It is not morality that compels us to return to the novel, but the spectacle of human life, the impression of its precariousness, and a vision of bitter tragedy bound to life's beauty.

3

Critical Reception

EARLY HISTORY

Tolstoy first planned to publish *Anna Karenina*, which he began in the spring of 1873, at his own expense. In 1874, he sent the first thirty-one chapters to the printer, and then decided not to publish. In November 1874, he agreed to have it serialized in the *Russian Messenger*. After the first four monthly installments (January to April 1875), work broke down. In 1876, five installments appeared (January through April), after which work broke down again until December. Four more installments appeared through the first four months of 1877; these contained the conclusion to part 7, Anna's suicide. The editor of the *Russian Messenger*, M. N. Katkov, refused to print the eighth part because Tolstoy ridiculed the volunteers' movement to help the Balkan Slavs, and Tolstoy published it in July as a separate booklet. *Anna Karenina* appeared in book form in January 1878.

The reading public was enthralled with the novel from the first issues of its serialization. N. N. Strakhov periodically reported to Tolstoy: "It is nothing less than delirium. I have seen solemn old men jumping up

and down in admiration" (13 February 1875); "Excitement keeps mount-
ing" (21 March 1875); "There is a roar of satisfaction as if you were
throwing food to starving men" (5 March 1876); "Everyone is taken up
with your novel. It's incredible how many people are reading it. Only
Gogol and Pushkin have ever been read like this" (February 1877)
(Knowles 1978, 25). Tolstoy also received enthusiastic letters from his
cousin, Countess A. A. Tolstaia, who described (June 1877) the endless
argument and gossip the novel was causing, and from his friend, the poet
A. A. Fet, who went into raptures over it.

But by and large, the reaction by the reviewers of the literary journals was an altogether different story. As Thomas Mann later reflected,
the critics "took in bad part Tolstoy's 'wilful remoteness from all contemporary *currents of progress*' " (1922, 143). One of the first to state his
objections (25 May 1875) was Turgenev: "I don't care for *Anna Karenina*,
although one comes across truly magnificent pages (the horse race, mowing, hunting). But it is all sour, with an odour of Moscow, incense, spin-
sterhood, the Slavophil thing and the gentry thing, etc." (Gifford 1971,
47). Many of the early reviewers, feeling shocked "at the sight of genius in
the camp of reaction" (Mann 1922, 144), turned facetious. V. G.
Avseenko said, "We are present at *the moment when the flow of life has
ceased*" (Knowles 1978, 262). A. M. Skabichevsky: "you start to sense
more and more the fragrance with which the novel is filled and which
forms its so to speak philosophic content. And do you know what this
fragrance is? (And one must admit it almost knocks one over.) It is that
distinctive smell you get on going into a nursery—the idyllic aroma of babies' nappies" (Knowles 1978, 266–67). P. N. Tkachov: "All the heroes of
the novel, all these Levins, Vronskys, Oblonskys, Annas, Dollies and Kit-
ties are characters who possess the material comforts, for whom, as a
consequence of the sort of upbringing they have had together with a
somewhat limited moral and intellectual development, the main 'duty for
the day' lies in their sexual relationships, interests and intrigues"
(Knowles 1978, 254). Looking back at this period of Tolstoy's life
Thomas Mann says, "The reactionary genius does occur, the brilliant and
conquering ability does act as attorney for retrograde tendencies—and

nothing dazes the world more than the sight of this paradoxical phenomenon" (1922, 144).[1]

Tolstoy's mockery of European progress alarmed the liberal intelligentsia, and this alarm underlies the satiric and acerbic criticism of *Anna Karenina*. The literary men found attitudes in the novel so offensive that it made it difficult if not impossible for them to read the novel as art. Tolstoy's reactionism and archaism represented to the liberal-radical camp superstition, inertia, and immorality, whereas they were on the side of justice, freedom, knowledge, and progress. Tkachov, after enunciating with as much mockery as he could summon the "artistic views" of Count Tolstoy, offered as a natural development of these views the following scenario as a sequel to *Anna Karenina*:

> Levin marries Kitty and lives with her in seclusion in the country, scorning all political and civic activity as fruitless and tedious concerns which lead to progress and civilization which themselves put a brake upon the growth of happiness. In a short period of time there appears in Levin's heart a more spontaneous and consequently more powerful and legitimate feeling than that of love for his wife: Levin experiences an agricultural love for his cow, Pava. Kitty notices her husband's new passion and seeing in it, because of her feminine frivolity, a certain danger to family happiness feels jealous and no longer wishes to look after Pava's calves as if they were her own children. (Knowles 1978, 259–60)

THE MARXIST VIEW

To Marxists, *Anna Karenina* is a historical document faithfully recording (along with the indelible stamp of the author's reactionary ideology) the transformation of old Russia by capitalism, which bureaucratized the ruling classes, destroying their humanity along with the masses they exploited.

Georg Lukács, the eminent Marxist theorist and writer on aesthetics, took as a starting point for his 1936 essay on Tolstoy (reprinted in *Studies in European Realism*, 1950) six essays by V. I. Lenin, particularly "Leo Tolstoy as the Mirror of the Russian Revolution" (1908) and "Lev

Tolstoi and his Epoch" (1911). Lenin read *Anna Karenina* as a document of the postemancipation period of Russian history when, as Tolstoy's hero Levin says, "Everything has now been turned upside down and is only just taking shape." Lenin writes that "it is difficult to imagine a more apt characterisation of the period 1861–1905. What 'was turned upside down' is familiar, or at least well known, to every Russian. It was serfdom, and the whole of the 'old order' that went with it. What 'is just taking shape' is totally unknown, alien and incomprehensible to the broad masses of the population. Tolstoi conceived this bourgeois order which was 'only just taking shape' vaguely" (1963, 17:49).

Lukács says that readers prior to Lenin quite missed this significance—that Tolstoy was the poetic mirror of an epoch in upheaval. "However wrong or reactionary his political and other opinions about this development may have been" (1950, 159), no one before him ever portrayed the inexorable division between the two nations in Russia, the peasants and the landowners, as vividly and palpably as he. Tolstoy—and this fact is made central—loathed capitalism and showed with remarkable subtlety how the expanding capitalistic transformation of postemancipation czarist Russia affects the personal life of his principal characters. Stiva, for instance, cannot live on the income from his estates. "The transition to closer ties with capitalism (a seat on a board of directors, etc.) is the natural consequence of his evolution, the natural widening of the new parasitic foundations of his life" (160). Vronsky, initially liberated by his passion for Anna, gives up his military prospects but then hardens into an enterprising landowner who "transforms the traditional husbandry of his estates into a capitalist enterprise, champions Liberalism and progress in the political counsels of the nobility and attempts to revive the 'independence' of the nobles' way of life on a capitalist basis" (163). Karenin, Lukács says, rounds off the picture. He is "the type of the already completely bureaucratized, reactionary, obscurantist, hypocritical and empty administrative official" (163).

The Lukács thesis is that, in *Anna Karenina*, "[c]apitalist division of labour increasingly permeates all human relationships, it becomes the way of life, the decisive determinant of thoughts and emotions" (1950, 163). This key to the novel, he says, was provided by V. I. Lenin, and

Lukács reiterates at the close of his essay that "[o]nly a Liberal or pseudo-Socialist vulgar-sociologist, who is infatuated with the capitalist form of progress, is capable of seeing only the reactionary aspects of this opposition, however desperate or blindly raging it may appear at times" (202).

The Soviet critic S. P. Bychkov, following the path of V. I. Lenin and Georg Lukács, handles Tolstoy's characters as if they were sticks for striking capitalism: "'A slow, delicate voice,' 'fixed dull eyes' and other physical details express Karenin's deadliness and the absence of any real life in him; this is not a person but a dummy, a wicked 'ministerial machine' busy making bureacratic circulars" (1970, 831). Anna, he says—stripping the novel of everything Tolstoy says of her inner psychology and dismissing all evidence that the novel has moral laws of its own—is not guilty; on the contrary, his Anna emerges as "the accuser of bourgeois-aristocratic society" (835). Tolstoy focuses attention on "the social causes of her tragic death" (835), by which Bychkov means the dehumanization, hypocrisy, and lies of capitalism, which crush Anna's truer and nobler feelings.

The Marxist response is remarkably narrow in dealing with Tolstoy's greatest character, as noted in chapter 6 in a more lengthy discussion of Lukács.

The All-Seeing Eye

Ivan Turgenev, Matthew Arnold, Dmitri Merejkowski, D. S. Mirsky, Virginia Woolf, Thomas Mann, Lionel Trilling, and Vladimir Nabokov are some of the writers who have sought to describe the universal qualities of Tolstoy's art. All of their interpretations are light-years from the Marxist notion of *Anna Karenina* as a sociopolitical document of an historical epoch. They marvel at Tolstoy's epic eye, a godlike, all-seeing illumination, which shines on everything with all-encompassing serenity. As Merejkowski says,

> In the works of Tolstoi there always, sooner or later, comes a moment when the reader finally forgets the main action of the story and the

fate of the principal characters. . . . [H]ow Kitty bears children, or Levin does his mowing, are to us so important and interesting that we lose sight of . . . Anna and Vronski. . . . In any case we feel no impatience, we are in no hurry to learn the ultimate fate of these persons. We are ready to wait, and have our attention distracted as much as the author likes. . . . As in every true epic there is nothing unimportant: everything is equally important, equally leading. In every drop there is the same salt taste, the same chemical composition of water as in the whole sea. Every atom of life moves according to the same laws as worlds and constellations. (1902, 244–45)

Merejkowski seems to imply, in the notion of Tolstoy understanding the laws of nature and the composition of life itself, an idea also implicit in Woolf and Mirsky—that Tolstoy, with his epic sweep and psychological penetration, is the Isaac Newton of belles lettres.

Woolf (1953, 185–86) says of Tolstoy: "Every twig, every feather sticks to his magnet. . . . And what his infallible eye reports of a cough or a trick of the hands his infallible brain refers to something hidden in the character so that we know his people, not only by the way they love and their views on politics and the immortality of the soul, but also by the way they sneeze and choke. Even in a translation we feel that we have been set on a mountain-top and had a telescope put into our hands. Everything is astonishingly clear and absolutely sharp."

Mirsky (1958, 263) says that Tolstoy puts into our hands not a telescope but a microscope. "An important form of this dissecting and atomizing method . . . is what Victor Shklovsky has called 'making it strange.' It consists in never calling complex things by their accepted name, but always disintegrating a complex action or object into its indivisible components. The method strips the world of the labels attached to it by habit and by social convention, and gives it a 'dis-civilized' appearance, as it might have appeared to Adam on the day of creation."

Mirsky also marvels at Tolstoy's penetration into the recesses of his characters' psyches (265). Tolstoy had a double eye (which Homer never had) that looked through his creations as if they were transparent, exposing their "semi-conscious suppressed motives" as clearly as he describes their features and actions. "He was . . . a rationalist to the marrow, one of the greatest that ever lived. Nothing was safe from the lancet of his analysis. His art is not the spontaneous revelation of the subconscious but the conquest of the subconscious by lucid under-standing. Tolstoy was a predecessor of Freud, but the striking dif-ference between the artist and the scientist is that the artist is incomparably less imaginative, more matter-of-fact and level-headed than the scientist."

Tolstoy is not Dostoyevsky, and my own tastes once inclined me to feel that this is the trouble with him: he seemed to lack a metaphysical system, the intellectual organization underlying the work of writers like Dostoyevsky and D. H. Lawrence. Many readers have just the opposite reaction. Nabokov, for instance, values nothing more highly than Tolstoy's power to create the impression of life, while he ranked Dostoyevsky as a second-rate artist with a penchant for melodrama and metaphysics. Merejkowski, Mann, and Steiner have written lengthy stud-ies analyzing the contrast between the two great contemporaries.

THE NOVEL'S MORAL VISION

One discovers the moral vision of *Anna Karenina* by interpreting the de-sign of the double plot and the narrator's point of view. What is the novel moving toward? What does the author believe? Tolstoy speaks directly through authorial comment and similes and indirectly through structure, that is, through what he calls the novel's "connections" or "links"—the points at which the two plots touch, characters are contrasted, etc. The action of the double plot contrasts the right and the wrong kind of love.

> While Anna is falling in love with Vronsky, Levin is being rejected by Kitty. When Kitty and Levin are falling in love, Anna is on her death-bed, attempting to reconcile herself to Karenin, struggling to give up Vronsky. As Anna and Vronsky leave Russia to begin their restless and aimless travels, Kitty and Levin are married. When Anna and Vronsky return to Moscow to make one desperate attempt to get a divorce and resolve their situation, Kitty is having a baby, finding new bonds of love and companionship with Levin. When Anna kills herself, Levin

finds the secret of life in the words of an ignorant peasant. By and large the novel describes the deterioration of Anna's and Vronsky's love and the growth toward maturity of Kitty's and Levin's love. (Wasiolek 1978, 150)

Dostoyevsky, whose interest in Tolstoy was never reciprocated (except for the *House of the Dead*, Tolstoy never wrote a generous word on his great contemporary), described (1877) the moral vision of *Anna Karenina* as if it were his own. He sees Anna as the great illustration of a doctrine that destroys the modern faith in progress: Evil is in the soul. Socialism and science are impotent physicians when it comes to relieving human misery. Only faith in God can do that. "[I]n the Russian author's approach to culpability and human delinquency it is clearly revealed that no [socialistic] ant-hill, no triumph of 'the fourth estate,' no elimination of poverty, no organization of labour will save mankind from abnormality, and therefore, from guilt and criminality. This is expressed in an immense psychological analysis of the human soul, with tremendous depth and potency, with a realism of artistic portrayal hitherto unknown in Russia" (Gifford 1971, 51–52).

Tolstoy, who never acknowledged Dostoyevsky's appreciation, reacted with delight to an article by M. S. Gromeka (1883): "[a]t last *Anna Karenina* has been explained!" (Eikhenbaum, *Seventies*, 138). Gromeka essentially agrees with Dostoyevsky that *Anna Karenina* aims a deathblow at the nineteenth century's faith in progress. But he goes one step further in attempting to define the moral laws of the novel, which he identifies with marriage and family.

It is impossible to destroy a family without creating unhappiness for it, and on this old unhappiness it is impossible to build new happiness. It is impossible to ignore public opinion entirely, because, even if it were incorrect, it is nevertheless an unavoidable condition of tranquility and freedom, and an open war with it envenoms, ulcerates, and cools the most ardent feeling. Marriage is nevertheless the only form of love in which a feeling calmly, naturally, and without hindrance forms durable bonds between people and society. . . . But this pure family principle can be created only on a stable foundation of true feeling. It cannot be built on external calculation. And a later infatuation with passion, like the natural consequence of an old lie, having destroyed it, will not correct anything and will lead only to final destruction because . . . "[v]engeance is mine; I will repay." (*Seventies*, 138–39)

Dostoyevsky and Gromeka emphasize the novel's didactic power: *Anna Karenina* advocates faith in God, belief in the family, and distrust of nineteenth-century intellectual pride, which, by seeking in science and economics laws governing human behavior, sought to supersede the old morality.

Boris Eikhenbaum, one of the most acclaimed of Tolstoy's critics, agrees in essence with Dostoyevsky and Gromeka that *Anna Karenina* is Tolstoy's "verdict on his times," but in Eikhenbaum's hands the novel is not a club for beating enemies so much as a resonant moral framework in which the featured story is about passion turning evil. He sees that Anna's compulsive destructiveness lies in passion itself, not because there is something intrinsically evil in passion, but because of "the 'evil spirit' which had settled in her"—her passion itself becoming the avenging agent of her conscience. Anna's bitterness "comes not from man, but from God'"—that is, from the sentence of her "own moral court ('eternal justice')" (*Seventies*, 146). Anna and Vronsky, he says, "both lead a life that is not real, because they follow only a narrowly understood 'will' or *desire*, not considering, as does Levin, the meaning of life. In this sense they are not real people, but slaves of their passion, of their egoism" (145).

Maire Jaanus Kurrik suggests that Levin is saved from nihilism because, unlike Anna, he has not been alienated from his body, which is Tolstoy's "very ground for the apprehension of God" (Bloom 1987, 106). Anna hates her body; she lives in guilty passion (perhaps in Tolstoy all erotic passion is guilty) and hence she never has such moments as Levin experiences when mowing—never feels the sensation of freedom from anxiety, a nonthinking, bodily feeling of joy. Without the support of such transcendental moments, Levin would have sunk into despair— the despair that Tolstoy feared and strove to defeat by conquering unclean desire and that he dramatizes through Anna, who "murders" her body with desire.

Richard Gustafson reads *Anna Karenina* as theology, as "verbal icons" of a religious world view. He contends that *all* of Tolstoy's narratives "tell of the divine call to love and man's response to that call," and that "[t]he history of Tolstoy's style is the story of his fiction becoming more and more emblematic" (1986, xii–xiii). *Anna Karenina*, he says, is a parable about the loss of faith and the search for God, in which Anna serves as a warning against self-indulgence and self-deception: "She is cast from a world of unconscious well-being into a world of conscious misery because in her pursuit of love she hides from her own truth. . . . Anna's truth is that in her way she does care for Karenin and her son. . . . Her story embodies and reveals the meaning of Tolstoy's words apparently spoken to Father Amvrosy, the elder at the famed monastery Optina Pustyn: 'When we are in God, i.e., in truth, then we are all together; when we are in the Devil, i.e., in falsehood, then we are all separate'" (132).[2]

ARTISTRY

R. F. Christian notes that "[f]or a long time it was the fashion to talk of the untidiness and sprawling nature of Tolstoy's and Dostoyevsky's novels, and to contrast their alleged shapelessness and formlessness with the harmony, economy and aesthetically satisfying order of Turgenev's" (1969, 129). This opinion was given a wide currency by Matthew Arnold and Henry James. As Arnold wrote:

> There are many characters in *Anna Karenine*—too many if we look in it for a work of art in which the action shall be vigorously one, and to that one action everything shall converge. There are even two main actions extending throughout the book, and we keep passing from one of them to the other. . . . People appear in connection with these two main actions whose appearance and proceedings do not in the least contribute to develop them; incidents are multiplied which we expect are to lead to something important, but which do not. What, for instance, does the episode of Kitty's friend Warinka and Levine's

brother Serge Ivanitch, their inclination for one another and its failure
to come to anything, contribute to the development of either the character or the fortunes of Kitty and Levine? (1888, 259–60)

This said, Arnold pens a memorable sentence, which influenced the
judgment of other critics: "But the truth is we are not to take *Anna
Karenine* as a work of art; we are to take it as a piece of life" (260). By this
he means that Tolstoy "has not invented and combined it, he has seen it;
it has all happened before his inward eye, and it was in this wise that it
happened. . . . The author saw it all happening so—saw it, and therefore
relates it; and what his novel in this way loses in art it gains in reality"
(260–61).

James favors writers who departed from the Victorian tradition of
the intrusive author in favor of Flaubert's attitude of narrative im-
personality, and he also adopts Flaubert's idea of artistic completeness in
the rendering of a single unified theme as superior to the multiplot novel.
In promoting these ends, he finds memorably expressive phrases—"fluid
pudding" (Gifford 1971, 105), for instance—to describe Tolstoy's novels. He complains, "but what do such large, loose, baggy monsters, with
their queer elements of the accidental and the arbitrary, artistically
mean?" (Knowles 1978, 434). On another occasion, somewhat more
charitably, he says, "Tolstoy is a reflector as vast as a natural lake; a monster harnessed to his great subject—all human life—as an elephant might
be harnessed, for purposes of traction, not to a carriage, but to a coach-
house. His own case is prodigious, but his example for others is dire: dis-
ciples not elephantine he can only mislead and betray" (Knowles 1978,
433).

But this criticism, while amusing, is not only biased against the Victorian novel, but is blind to the artistry of *Anna Karenina*. Recent studies
by Stenbock-Fermor, Schultze, Thorlby, and Armstrong on the aesthetic
complexity of the novel's architectonics; by Christian and Bayley on
Tolstoy's conscientious art, his will to Style, as James might say; and by
Eikhenbaum, Nabokov, and Wasiolek on his use of symbolism, images,
and motifs, have superseded Arnold's and James's criticisms. From the
table-tapping introduced in part 1 at the Shcherbatsky's to Anna's

shocked sight of the peasant, her old nightmare figure, shortly before she kills herself, Tolstoy works through his long narrative a dark strand of telepathy, forebodings, and doubles, which adds tautness as well as tragic inevitability to Anna's story. He situates events of crisis and tragedy on trains six times through the course of his novel. This association of trains with tragedy gives a structural unity to the novel and also serves as an illustration of his hero's hatred of civilization. Bad things are brought to Russia on trains from the West.

But these are small effects compared to the chief thing. The poetic complexity of the novel lies in the touch points between the two plots, in the patterning of the segments of chapters, in the contrast between characters and actions, in the rhyming of recurring situations, the "connections" or "links." On 23 and 26 April 1876 he wrote to N. N. Strakhov:

> But if I were to try to say in words everything that I intended to express in my novel, I would have to write the same novel I wrote from the beginning. And if short-sighted critics think that I only wanted to describe the things that I like, what Oblonsky has for dinner or what Karenina's shoulders are like, they are mistaken. In everything, or nearly everything I have written, I have been guided by the need to gather together ideas which for the purpose of self-expression were interconnected; but every idea expressed separately in words loses its meaning and is terribly impoverished when taken by itself out of the connection in which it occurs. The connection itself is made up, I think, not by the idea, but by something else, and it is impossible to express the basis of this connection directly in words. It can only be expressed indirectly—by words describing characters, actions and situations. . . . [p]eople are needed for the criticism of art who can show the pointlessness of looking for ideas in a work of art and can steadfastly guide readers through that endless labyrinth of connections which is the essence of art, and towards those laws that serve as the basis of these connections. (*Tolstoy's Letters* 1978, 1:296–97)

4

History, Ideology, Fiction: Tolstoy from 1860 to 1880

A Rural Schoolteacher

Tolstoy was a young literary lion in 1856—author of *Childhood* (1852), *Boyhood* (1854), and the *Sevastopol Sketches* (1855–56). The literary journals praised him "for his great ability as a painter of pictures, the charm, vigour, concision and poetry of his style, his great powers of observation and the capacity to use them, his extremely acute psychological analysis, his honesty and straightforwardness and scorn for literary effects for their own sake and for the fact that he wrote about people and events as they really were" (Knowles 1978, 18). Turgenev recorded his impressions of Tolstoy at this time: "He's a strange man and I can't quite understand him. A mixture of poet, Calvinist, fanatic and landowner's son; somewhat reminiscent of Rousseau, but more honest; highly moral but at the same time not someone you can warm to" (Turgenev 1983, 65).

But by the late 1850s Tolstoy was out of favor. The Germanophile czar, Nicholas I, who had stood as a guardian of conservatism, died in 1855. Aroused by Alexander II's promises of reform, radical critics, led by Nikolay Chernyshevsky, clamored for books reflecting the social problems of the day. New dicta arose as to what the writer's role should be. Soon the major Russian liberal journals, applying the credo, "the time for belles lettres has now passed" (*Tolstoy's Letters* 1978, 1:112), ignored fictional works that were not "timely." Tolstoy was unable to adapt to his colleagues' form of social art, and *Youth* (1857), *Lucerne* (1857), *Albert* (1858), and "Three Deaths" (1859) met with disfavor. "[H]e was accused of being old-fashioned, tendentious and didactic, he often took his psychological analysis to perverse lengths, his outlook on life tended to be purely negative, he suffered from an over-detailization, his stories had no plot or action and his use of the Russian language left much to be desired" (Knowles 1978, 18–19).

Tolstoy feared that he would have to give up writing and not altogether because he felt superior to the so-called propaganda novel: he began to lose faith in his own creativity. In 1859 he chose to settle on his estate at Yasnaya Polyana and occupy himself with farming. However, by the fall, he had found a way of engaging himself in ideological combat that, in retrospect, seems to have led him back to literature. He had set up a free public school for peasant children on his estate.

Tolstoy was influenced by the *Russian Messenger*'s propagandizing of the German populist Wilhelm Riehl (1823–97), whose theories were directed against the teachings of Marx. Plans were in the air for freeing the serfs (this occurred on 19 February 1861), and enmity between the classes had become an acutely pressing issue. In Count Tolstoy's social sphere, Riehl's works were timely because they showed a way out of this enmity. The polemicist of the *Russian Messenger*, Bezobrazov, applying Riehl's theories to an analysis of class in Russia, warned against forming a proletariat out of the peasantry, because any proletariat "is formed from elements which are disintegrating the political order" (Eikhenbaum, *Sixties*, 35). Russia is unique, he wrote, in that it has "only two substantial social groups . . . the landowners and the peasants. . . . The landowning class, and, in general, the aristocracy, is a higher stage in the development of the peasantry. The landowner . . . is a peasant who has realized his potential." Bezobrazov claimed that no class other than the aristocracy showed real sympathy for the peasantry and that once the landowning class "stops thinking about its regrettable ancestral privileges, and starts thinking about its high social calling," harmony and stability would be assured (35).

Tolstoy, along with the Slavophiles, adopted Riehl's views. The West must not be imitated. "The social theories of recent times are all nonsense because they deny the historical . . . (fact), the ethnic soil, the organic principle of life in general" (Eikhenbaum, *Sixties*, 41) preserved in the peasantry.[3] Society needed to be recreated and renewed, but not by revolution: "the peasantry constitutes the conservative element in the state, and . . . therefore, first and foremost, the position of the peasants must be raised, its characteristic features must be preserved, its needs satisfied. The peasant reestablished the balance in society which was destroyed by the unnatural development of civilization. Socialism can not be defeated now by the press, or by government measures, but it can be overcome with the help of the peasantry, by carefully preserving their values and traditions" (45).[4]

Tolstoy's becoming a teacher of peasant children was an original public statement—his way of defining a political position vis-à-vis the crucial issues of his time, something he was not yet able to do in his fiction.

In order to formulate his position on what peasants should be taught and how, Tolstoy traveled to France, Belgium, England, and Germany (July 1860–May 1861). He found the German people spoiled by false education that perverted the traditions and outlook of the peasantry. He went abroad determined to prove a cardinal tenet, and proved it—that "[e]very abstract method introduced into the system is an illusion" (Eikhenbaum, *Sixties*, 25).[5]

Tolstoy's school at Yasnaya Polyana sought to preserve peasant traditions. It was located in a small, two-story building next to the main house. The children brought no books with them. They sat where they liked, on the floor, on the tables. They were free to come and go. Discipline was imposed by those who were attentive. "The lessons," Troyat writes, "if these casual chats between an adult and some children could be called that" were lengthy, undisciplined, and shallow and ranged "from grammar to carpentry, by way of religious history, singing, geography, gymnastics, drawing and composition" (1967, 216).[6]

Tolstoy publicized his school and educational theory in twelve issues of a periodical, *Yasnaya Polyana* (January–December 1862), which he distributed to about 400 subscribers. In one of the first issues, he declared that peasants must remain peasants. "The public education for which rural teachers are being prepared is madness, the product of the old leveling principle of rationalism. There can be no such thing as public education. . . . The village teacher is needed not in order to realize some pedagogical theory but in order to help the peasant become a true peasant" (Eikhenbaum, *Sixties*, 52).

In a letter dated 7 August 1862 he claimed that university students who came to teach at his school were cured of the intelligentsia's revolutionary notions and within a week were teaching "Bible history and prayers, and handed round the Gospels for reading at home" (*Tolstoy's Letters* 1978, 1:161).

Tolstoy argued indignantly in a journal article that the principal evil of education was the "repudiation of home." So-called enlightened teachers perverted children with notions aimed at developing them, and their parents "look with even greater amazement and grief at their emaciated, self-assured, and self-satisfied Vania who speaks an alien language, thinks with a foreign mind, smokes cigarettes, and drinks wine" (Eikhenbaum, *Sixties*, 56).

The important historical meaning of the Yasnaya Polyana school is that it served Tolstoy as a bridge back to writing; it was primarily a learning experience for him, a laboratory in which he formed himself ideologically.[7]

MARRIAGE

In September 1862, Tolstoy married Sofia Andreyevna Behrs. She was not quite nineteen and had earned a university diploma qualifying her as a private teacher. Her father was a Moscow physician working for the administrative staff of the imperial palace. Tolstoy proposed to Sofia, as recorded in Sofia's younger sister's memoirs, just as Levin proposes to Kitty in *Anna Karenina*, a scene in which something approaching thought-reading took place. Sitting at a card table with Sofia, Tolstoy wrote on a chalkboard the initial letters of the sentence, "Your youth and your thirst for happiness remind me cruelly of my age and the impossibility of happiness for me" (Troyat 1967, 239). Sofia guessed right. The thirty-four-year-old man, stocky, heavily bearded, with a crooked nose and iron grey eyes, and missing nearly all his teeth, felt his happiness was assured, and the marriage took place the following week.

Tolstoy discontinued his school shortly after returning to Yasnaya Polyana with his bride, and by December of 1863 had returned to writing fiction, waging his fight against the new literary ideas and dicta as an artist rather than a pedagogue. In this work he found that he had been remarkably lucky in his choice of a wife.

The first year of marriage was very hard for Sofia Andreyevna. She had nothing to do in the country. Tolstoy was busy managing the estate, and she was bored. The difficulty between them was exacerbated by their mania for showing each other their diaries, a practice begun before their marriage when Tolstoy insisted (like Levin later) on her reading his old diaries, which were filled with unsavory details of his bachelor life. Troyat caustically comments that Sofia was "marked for life by that desecration" (1967, 249). She found out about his affair with a peasant woman, Aksinya, who continued to live at Yasnaya Polyana as a house servant. Sofia was inflamed with jealousy. Tolstoy, for his part, reproached her repeatedly for idleness and frigidity; "doll" was his pejorative nickname for her. "They could hardly have striven more mightily to bare their naked souls if their chief object had been to become thoroughly disgusted with each other" (262).

The chief difficulty was Tolstoy's restlessness with himself. He was in the trough between his work with the peasant children and his work on *War and Peace* (begun in December 1863).[8] His diary for 18 June 1863 reads, "In the intoxication of estate management I've ruined nine irretrievable months which could have been the best of my life, but which I made almost the worst. . . . It's awful, terrible and absurd to link one's happiness with material conditions—a wife, children, health, wealth" (*Tolstoy's Diaries* 1985, 1:178). Even more bitter are Prince Andrew's words to Pierre in *War and Peace*: "Marry when you are old and good for nothing—or all that is good and noble in you will be lost. It will all be wasted on trifles. . . . If you marry expecting anything from yourself in the future, you will feel at every step that for you all is ended, all is closed" (*War and Peace* 1966, 1:2).

The family trauma was largely overcome when Tolstoy took up the pen to actually begin work on his great historical novel. Sofia took upon herself all the household responsibilities—the management of the estate, the accounts, the education of their children (eight children were born in the first eleven years of their marriage)—and saw to it that no one disturbed her husband while he was writing. She was, as well, his devoted copyist.

WAR AND PEACE

Like the diaries, which Tolstoy began in 1847 and which can be regarded as exercises in style, the school at Yasnaya Polyana helped him solve the problems of his life and his writing. The peasant boys Semka and Fedka, in his educational article "Who Should Learn to Write from Whom, the Peasant Children from Us, or We from the Peasant Children?" represent two artistic methods.

> Semka seemed to see and describe whatever happened to be in front of him: a pair of stiff, frozen bast shoes and the dirt which dripped off them when they were thawing out, and the charred husks they became when the old woman threw them into the fire . . . Fedka saw the snow filling up the old man's foot cloths and the compassion with which the peasant said: "Oh Lord, how far he must have walked!" (In depicting characters, Fedka would even show how the peasant looked when he said this, waving his arms and nodding his head.) He saw the coat sewn together out of rags and the torn shirt, beneath which the old man's body was visible, soaked by the melting snow. (Eikhenbaum, *Sixties*, 67–68)

When *The Cossacks* appeared in 1863 Tolstoy was attacked for lacking a social conscience—for never giving thought "to the unequal distribution of social elements or to the causes of this inequality" (Eikhenbaum,

Sixties, 89)—and, as one of the bankrupt writers of the old style, for having left life behind to squander his energies on trifles and details. Tolstoy feared the realistic tendency embodied by Semka: too much description, too many details without an underlying idea. Throughout his life he questioned the meaning of existence—scourging himself for lust in his diaries, driving himself with self-censure, and despairing at failing to find sooner the rational and moral justifications, which eventually led to his religious conversion. Thus the Fedka in Tolstoy's artistic temperament increasingly became a force that, by the time *Anna Karenina* was written, was equal to the realist. After *Anna Karenina* the moral impulse represented by Fedka became dominant, and he subordinated his artistic powers to accommodating his religious message in works that were not only stories and pictures but extended parables based on folk sayings.

Turgenev regretted Tolstoy's moralizing tendency, which he regarded as an ideological blight, the substitution of shallow abstractions for deep perceptions. Turgenev considered *The Cossacks* as a chef d'oeuvre and exclaimed over Tolstoy's ability to capture life. Similarly, Nabokov found Tolstoy's art, his descriptive power (Semka), astonishing: "so tiger bright, so original and universal" (1981, 138). There has been no greater writer, he says, than "the man who gloated over the beauty of black earth, white flesh, blue snow, green fields, purple thunderclouds" (140). In "those great chapters that are his masterpieces," Nabokov says, the tendency to sacrifice the giant that he was to the philosopher that he had chosen to become (Fedka) is "invisible" (143).

The ideological content of *War and Peace*, so tame to modern readers, was reactionary in its time, opposed to all the liberal ideals of the French Revolution and the nineteenth century (progress, rationalism, materialism). It defended the natural, immutable qualities of nature that the imposition of civilized values spoils and destroys. Tolstoy glorifies everything Russian, that is, everything identified with nature—impulsive courage, intuitive wisdom—in short, natural man. His ideal in *War and Peace* is the old hereditary, landowning gentry—men who lived like their fathers and forefathers, with strong family ties, close paternal relationships with their peasants, and a general Christian ethic. Indeed, he looked with suspicion at everything in Russia that postdates Peter the Great and chose to write about Napoleon's invasion in order to celebrate the domestic life of people that endures unchanged by cataclysms of war and so-called progress.

Tolstoy chose to write a historical novel with the intention of being antihistorical—to demonstrate that nothing could be discovered by social observation and historical inference and that the so-called great man of history was nothing more than an "epiphenomenon of a process which would have occurred unaltered without him" (Berlin 1967, 34).

In his readings he was particularly attracted to Joseph De Maistre (1753–1821), who was a violent antihumanist. When in Moscow and working on the theoretical chapters of *War and Peace*, Tolstoy associated with a reactionary circle of learned friends who were distrustful of scientific methods and opposed to the influence of rationalism and liberalism so pervasive in Western Europe.[9]

In the theoretical chapters of *War and Peace*, Tolstoy argues that it is impossible to ascertain the ultimate and sufficient cause of any historical event. All historical events are infinitely complex, representing the sum and integration of countless human actions over a long period of time, and widely dispersed in space. Such is the complexity of the causation of large-scale events, like Napoleon's invasion of Russia, that they can easily appear to be inevitable. Man "is at once an atom living its own conscious life 'for itself', and at the same time the unconscious agent of some historical trend, a relatively insignificant element in the vast whole composed of a very large number of such elements" (Berlin 1967, 32–33). Therefore, a person cannot cause historical events, since nothing begins with an individual act. One must seek not specific causes, but laws which govern phenomena. However, neither the causes of history nor the laws governing history can be determined, because people live in history and cannot step out of it: "one can know—really know—only one's own point in time and space. The more limited man becomes, the more real he becomes and the more effective he becomes in discerning the direction of reality. . . . One becomes conscious of the world to the extent that one permits it to rise in one's consciousness, and one permits it to rise in one's consciousness to the extent that one withdraws one's control over the world, whether the control is one of command, judgment, wish" (Wasiolek 1978, 123, 125).

Tolstoy attacks principled goodness and benevolence as naive and ineffective and affirms the instinctive life rather than the intellectual. In the scene at Bogucharovo, Andrey scoffs at Pierre's efforts at reform—at educating the peasants and lightening their load. Andrey, the pragmatist, speaking as Levin will later, says that actions derived from intellectual principles are worthless. Charity—that is, reform made in adherence to an ideal—disregards the actual circumstances at hand and thus is ineffective and even harmful. Pierre's progressive notions of education would destroy the peasants' animal happiness. Andrey succeeds in improving the peasants' lot because his assistance is always mingled with self-interest (Wasiolek 1978, 75).

The sacramental scenes in the novels are luminous—for example, Nicholas at the wolf hunt and Levin mowing with the peasants. These moments are "openings, as it were, in that ordinary life through which there came glimpses of something sublime. And in the contemplation of this sublime something the soul was exalted to inconceivable heights of which it had before had no conception, while reason lagged behind, unable to keep up with it" (7:14). At these transcendent moments the will is submerged and the individual experiences a sensation of oneness with the whole of creation.

As Isaiah Berlin says in his study of *War and Peace*, to Tolstoy harmony with life is, above all, "not anything that art, or science or civilization or rational criticism can achieve" (Berlin 1967, 76). For this reason, the novel aroused Turgenev's indignation. *War and Peace*, he writes, "is constructed on opposition to intelligence, knowledge and consciousness" (1983, 172–73). Berlin suggests that Tolstoy's reactionism is an expression of his moral drive, a nihilistic impatience with theories that do not give a moral framework to existence. Torn by conflict between reason and a passionate desire for a monistic vision of life, Tolstoy strikes out at nineteenth-century intellectual ideas, using his deterministic theory of history as a bludgeon.

THE SLOUGH OF DESPOND

Today the Soviets have elevated *War and Peace* beyond criticism, but the reception of the novel in the 1860s was very different. Professional criticism, mired in the puddle of contemporary issues, was blind to its epic grandeur. The radicals condemned Tolstoy as an extreme reactionary, criticizing the novel on two main counts: "[I]n idealizing the nobility he had not depicted the intelligentsia and in praising the landowners he had not attacked serfdom" (Knowles 1978, 23). Military men denounced him for not describing battles accurately. With the exception of the Slavophiles, who declared Tolstoy their hero, criticism of the theoretical chapters was most severe. Turgenev mourned Tolstoy's tendency to "mutilate his own handiwork" (Maude 1930, 1:332). Tolstoy, with the assistance of N. N. Strakhov, hastily and radically revised his novel in 1873. Many of the historical and philosophical discourses were taken out of the basic text and put in a special appendix.[10]

Tolstoy, having completed *War and Peace*, experienced great restlessness. He shut himself up in Yasnaya Polyana and ceased to receive either newspapers or periodicals, outraged by the magazine reviews of his novel. In the gloomy summer of 1869, immersed in reading Schopenhauer, he showed signs of psychic disorder, and his wife's diaries and letters show him to be painfully ill with depression. On 9 December 1870 she wrote: "Sometimes it seemed to him—this occurred to him always away from home and away from the family—that he would go out of his mind, and the fear of madness grew so strong that later, when he would tell me about this, I would be overcome with horror" (Eikhenbaum, *Seventies*, 30–31).

Sofia is alluding to Tolstoy's experience at a hotel in Arzamas in September 1869, when he was overcome by a horrifying presentiment of his death. It came upon him suddenly, and, as he describes it ten years later in an unfinished, fictionalized account, the *Diary of a Madman*, it changed his life. "There was left in my mind a horrible residue as if some misfortune had befallen me which I could only temporarily forget, and which remained there in the back of my mind and took possession of me. . . . I began to live as before, but the fear of that anguish hung over me from that time onwards" (Lavrin, ed., 1946, 159–60). In the autumn of 1871, S. A. Tolstaya wrote her sister, "Levochka is constantly saying that all is over for him, that he will die soon, nothing makes him happy, that there is nothing more to expect from life" (Eikhenbaum, *Seventies*, 31).

In the winter of 1870, Tolstoy studied Greek with phenomenal concentration. After three months he was reading Herodotus. The contradiction between the Greek outlook and his own at this period depressed him. To the Greeks, "religion places the meaning of life in earthly happiness, in beauty and in strength" (Maude 1930, 1:327). Their art powerfully transmits the joy and energy of life in the here and now. And what else, above all, did *War and Peace* advocate but the easy, vivid, brilliant discovery of life? "[W]ithout a knowledge of Greek there is no education," Tolstoy wrote to A. A. Fet (*Tolstoy's Letters* 1978, 1:231), but in his troubled mental state after *War and Peace* he "hated his own vital bearish strength," because he was "straining away from nature, naivete, moral indifference . . . towards moral valuations and edifying doctrine" (Mann, "Anna Karenina," 180).[11]

Eikhenbaum suggests yet another cause for his anguished mood after completing *War and Peace*. This was the popular acclaim for N. Flerovsky (a pseudonym for Vasilii Vasilievich Berv), an old classmate at the University of Kazan, whose *The Condition of the Working Class in Russia* (1869) was directed against the aristocratic paternalism that was dear to Tolstoy. Flerovsky rejected the notion that Russia had no proletariat. On the contrary, he proved with statistics that workers in Russia, in comparison with those in Western Europe, were deplorably worse off, that "Russia is a country of prevailing pauperism, that all the benefits obtained by the people through their communal ownership of the land and independent economy are being completely obliterated by their being held in suppression and by their ignorance" (*Seventies*, 21). Eikhenbaum notes that Marx extolled Flerovsky's book as the most important book next to Engels's *The Condition of the Working Class in England* (*Seventies*, 165 n. 21), and that it made a greater impression on the men of the 1870s than did *War and Peace*. Flerovsky was a powerful influence on the intelligentsia, and Tolstoy could not help respecting him: "The image of this free wanderer, tied neither by family nor property . . . a person whom no one could dare reproach with preaching one thing and doing another—this image apparently haunted both the imagination and conscience of Tolstoi" (*Seventies*, 27).

In the period of restlessness and depression between *War and Peace* and *Anna Karenina*, Tolstoy engaged in two campaigns against the liberal intelligentsia. Public education had become the main point of the class struggle in the 1870s. The questions of what children were to be taught, by whom, and under whose administration were causes of anxiety to the landowning aristocracy, whose economic and political welfare required control over the masses. Tolstoy, despising the liberalizing nobility as well as the revolutionary intelligentsia, defended his interests by developing a complete course in elementary education and by publicly attacking progressive pedagogy. As early as the summer of 1869, he began to read Russian folktales and epics with the intention of creating an anthology of readings for four age groups, beginning with a primer. "My proud dreams about this *Primer* are," he wrote to his cousin A. A. Tolstaya in January 1872, "that two generations of *all* Russian children, from tsars' to peasants', will study with the aid of this *Primer* alone, and will receive their first poetic impressions from it" (*Letters* 1978, 1:240–41).

Tolstoy's *Primer*, published in 1872, was "not at all about methods of teaching literacy, but about the understanding of what 'the people' is and of what the obligations of the intelligentsia were to this 'people'" (Eikhenbaum, *Seventies*, 41). Students were to be taught faith and moral rules, and the stories in the *Primer* and the *Russian Readers* emphasized developing the moral element before the mental. Almost all of them "were imbued with resignation to fate, with trust in blind chance, with fatalism" (56). Tolstoy's ideal of a public school had its origin in the older educational practices: "Small schools in homes, without any scientific 'German' frills, without any views, methods, and theories, without any natural sciences, history, and geography—with reading and writing, with arithmetic, and with sacred history" (45). The *Primer* and the *Russian Readers*, regarded by the intelligentsia as reactionary phenomena, met with fairly general acceptance and were widely used in the nation's schools.[12]

The question of the fate of the old landowning aristocracy, which Tolstoy still considered in the seventies to be the social base of Russia, had him studying the age of Peter the Great through the fall and winter of 1872–73. "Russian scientific historiography was born of the polemics of the Westernizers with the Slavophiles, and the central point of these polemics was the question of the role of Peter I" (Eikhenbaum, *Seventies*, 69). Tolstoy contemplated a historical novel that would attack Peter's centralized state system and his reform of old patriarchal and communal Rus into modern Russia. He would use his literary genius to raise the old Russian commune to the level of a moral ideal. Despite the publication in 1863 of Solovev's voluminous historical work, which made nonsense of the Slavophiles' conception of history, and despite Flerovsky's systematic attack on the self-serving propaganda of agrarian paternalism, Tolstoy planned his novel to glorify the ideal of the old Russian commune and to show how old Rus was infected by Western ideas.

Tolstoy belonged to the old hereditary nobility who lived on their country estates. His farming enterprise consisted of "300 [pigs] paired off in separate styes ... 80 cows, 500 good sheep, and very many fowls" (Maude 1930, 1:319). He had estates as well in the distant Samaran province where he bred horses. Paternalism among agrarian gentry like the Tolstoys "was conceived as the landowner's moral responsibility for the fate of his peasants—implying both the right to exert paternal authority over them and the duty to show them paternal care, to help them in case of need and to make a just settlement of controversial questions." This gentry "regarded themselves and their peasants as members of one community, almost of one family. Of course, this was only 'ideology,' but it was held with equal sincerity by both sides which made it possible in many instances to tone down conflicts" (Walicki 1975, 182).

Tolstoy was to undergo a revolution in his beliefs after the writing of *Anna Karenina*, when this paternal ideal would be swept away as anathema. But in *Anna Karenina*, Levin's theory of agriculture is based on this ideology, as is his tirade against Vronsky, who represents a type of the "modern" court nobility Tolstoy despised: "No, excuse me, but I consider myself aristocratic, and people like me, who can point back in the past to three or four honorable generations of their family, of the highest degree of breeding . . . and have never curried favor with anyone" (2:17).

Indeed, Tolstoy gives the full force of moral sanction to the patriarchal code of the "aristocrat" in his dealings with the peasants. Levin, in fact, enumerates a lengthy code of obligations and responsibilities for his peasants, distinguishing between practical claims and sentimental ones. This ideology is also apparent, as Eikhenbaum notes, in the way "Levin, with his muzhiks who know better and more thoroughly than any philosopher how and why one has to live, is consistently contrasted with the representatives of all other classes and strata" (*Seventies*, 55).

ANNA KARENINA

> And what truths can there be, if there is death?
> —Gorky, *Reminiscences of Leo Nikolaevich Tolstoy*, 45

As far back as 24 February 1870, the idea of writing a novel about adultery had flashed across Tolstoy's mind. S. A. Tolstaya noted at that time in her diary that he had conceived the character of a woman, married, of high society who had "lost her way." He said that his task was to make this woman "only pitiable and not guilty" (Eikhenbaum, *Seventies*, 144). When suddenly in 1873 he dropped his plan of an historical novel on the age of Peter the Great, the earlier notion of a novel about adultery came to mind. It was reinforced by an occurrence that had deeply affected him the previous year. His neighbor had a mistress whom he abandoned for his children's governess. The mistress, whose name was Anna, threw herself under a freight train, leaving a note for her ex-lover in which she called him her murderer and invited him to see her corpse on the tracks at Yasenki. The day after her suicide, Tolstoy went to the station. "Standing in a corner of the shed, he had observed every detail of the woman's body lying on the table, bloody and mutilated, with its skull crushed" (Troyat 1967, 344).

Tolstoy's attitude toward the role of women was hostile and static throughout the debates of the 1860s and 1870s, when the question of women's rights became "one of the most topical and militant themes of Russian journalists and writers of fiction" (Eikhenbaum, *Seventies*, 95). His comedy farce *A Contaminated Family* (1864) derides the emancipation of women, and in the epilogue to *War and Peace*, his ideal of "family happiness" is presented through the stultifying marriage of Natasha and Pierre. Steiner, in reflecting on this domestic bliss, speaks of the inherent smallness of their relationship, emphasizing Natasha's stinginess, untidiness, stoutness, querulous jealousy, "ferocious standards of monogamy," and "utter absorption in the details of childbearing and family life" (1959, 110). Nevertheless, Tolstoy's moral position is plain: "Man's mission—men are the worker bees of the hive of human society—is endlessly diverse, but the mission of the queen bee, without whom reproduction of the species is impossible, is without question one and the same. . . . The more she goes into it, the more this mission will absorb her altogether and appear limitless to her" (Eikhenbaum, *Seventies*, 96). Therefore, the happily married Natasha Bezukhov has no interest in women's rights and is content with being "rather mussy and unfresh" (Lawrence 1963, 112). She is totally and rightly absorbed in breeding.

N. N. Strakhov's critical review of John Stuart Mill's *The Subjection of Women* was enthusiastically embraced by Tolstoy. Strakhov's conclusion was that "for the majority of married women it is impossible to devote themselves to other matters except *the simple duties of the housewife and mother of the family*" (Eikhenbaum, *Seventies*, 97). In his letter to Strakhov commending his review, Tolstoy raised the rhetorical question, And what about women who have not found a husband, or have already borne their children? To which he answers, "if we will just not believe that the social structure came about by the will of some fools and evil people, as does Mill, but by a will incomprehensible to us, then the place occupied in it by the nonfamily woman will be clear to us," (99) namely, that all such women should become "*nannies*—in the very widest folk sense" (98).

Tolstoy found support for his position against the progressive Russian press particularly in a treatise by Alexandre Dumas fils, *L'Homme-femme*, which appeared in 1872. Dumas raises the question of how to act towards an unfaithful wife, and its concluding pages, addressed to an imaginary son, delighted Tolstoy with its forthrightness.

> And now if, in spite of your precautions . . . your virtue, your patience, and your kindness, if you have been deceived . . . if you have joined to your life a creature unworthy of you, if after having vainly tried to make her the wife she ought to be, you have not been able to save her through maternity, that earthly redemption of her sex; if, wishing no longer to listen to you neither as a husband, nor as a father, nor as a friend, nor as a teacher, she not only abandons your children but goes off with the first man she meets and brings other children into the world . . . if the law, which has taken upon itself the right to tie together has refused itself the right to untie and declares itself helpless, declare yourself . . . the judge and the executioner of this creature. She is not . . . a woman . . . she is simply animal, she is the monkey from the Biblical land of Nod, she is Cain's female;—kill her. (Eikhenbaum, *Seventies*, 102–3)

Tolstoy wrote about Dumas's *L'Homme-femme* enthusiastically to his sister-in-law: "One would never have expected a Frenchman to have such a lofty understanding of marriage or of the relationships in general between a man and a woman" (Christian 1969, 168).

Some readers, like Maksim Gorki, point to Tolstoy's "implacable hostility" toward women who are too sexual. "It is the hostility of the male who has not succeeded in getting all the pleasure he could, or it is the hostility of spirit against 'the degrading impulses of the flesh.' But it is hostility, and cold as in *Anna Karenina*" (1920, 18–19).

In the original plan of the novel the principal tragic character was to be Anna's husband who, in an extant early draft, really loves her and suffers deeply. Originally Karenin was portrayed as "a kindly, rather dreamy, magnanimous gentleman, a 'scholarly eccentric,' trying with sincere Christian fortitude to endure a disaster which had overtaken him through no fault of his own." Anna was at first "unattractive, vulgar, coquettish, stout and even ugly" (Christian 1969, 170). The plan was to follow Dumas's book, "disagreeing only with his final conclusion: 'kill her'" (Eikhenbaum, *Seventies*, 114). However, the appearance of Levin in the scheme (the Levin-Kitty plot was an afterthought) radically changed Tolstoy's original concept. The inclusion of Levin, the landowner with one foot firmly rooted in nature, influenced the treatment of Karenin "through lowering his image and turning him into a typical bureaucrat-official; a natural result of this lowering was the elevating of Anna, since Karenin could and should no longer play a tragic role" (114).

By 1875, Tolstoy found the work on *Anna Karenina* difficult to sustain, and until it was completed in the spring of 1877, his letters and diaries indicate that he was struggling with it as if against his will.

A number of psychological explanations have been given for Tolstoy's aversion to his novel. Wasiolek argues that in his treatment of Anna, Tolstoy was confronting an idea inimical to him—that sexual love could be a corrupting power. His philosophy in *War and Peace* had been that whatever is innate and instinctive is good. Discovering that physical passion is degrading and destructive appalled Tolstoy, reversing his belief that the source of evil was external. "If then Anna's fate has not been caused by the corrupting influences around her, then the physical passion must have another source. But if the physical passion and its destructive attributes are something innate, something given, then they must be something in the order of nature. If this is so, then much of Tolstoy's edifice comes crashing down. . . . Tolstoy in the writing of *Anna Karenina* is at the point of a truly tragic stance, the acknowledgment that evil exists and is inextirpable from human nature" (Wasiolek 1978, 131).

Gifford attributes Tolstoy's aversion to guilt. He says "[i]t becomes very clear that he finds [Anna's] lawless passion deeply disturbing. A conscience as strict as Tolstoy's must have been aware that the long drawn-out imagining of this beautiful woman's predicament was a kind of infidelity to his own wife: hence the outbursts of disgust with the novel" (1982, 40).

Mann finds the roots of Tolstoy's difficulty in his obsession with death. At this time it demanded "spiritual wrestling, not in a literary way but in something confessional on the pattern of Saint Augustine and Rousseau. Such a book, sincere as far as human power could make it, weighed on his mind and gave him increasing distaste for writing novels" ("Anna Karenina," 183).

History, Ideology, Fiction: Tolstoy from 1860 to 1880

Tolstoy's work on the novel coincided with his inner struggle that ended with *Confession* in 1879. There was an acute period in his emotional state, beginning in 1875, when the thought of death did not leave him. S. A. Tolstaya's diary entry for 12 October 1875 reads, "It's painful for me to see him when he is like this, despondent and dejected for days and weeks on end, neither working nor writing, without energy or joy, just as though he had become reconciled to this condition" (Sophia Tolstoy 1985, 52). In February 1876, he wrote to his brother, "Nothing more remains in life but to die." In March 1876 he wrote his cousin A. A. Tolstaya that he was tormented by his preoccupation with death, but could find no solution in philosophy or religion, and in April he wrote to her, "With the demands of my mind and the answers given by the Christian religion, I find myself in the position, as it were, of two hands endeavouring to clasp each other while the fingers resist. I long to do it, but the more I try, the worse it is" (*Letters* 1978, 1:296). He wrote to A. A. Fet that his obsession with death had become part of the installment that had recently appeared in the April issue of the *Russian Messenger*.

This installment, describing the death of Levin's brother, was based on the deaths of Tolstoy's brothers, Dmitri and Nikolay, of tuberculosis (1856 and 1860)—a disease that Tolstoy always feared. Between 1873 and 1875 he was surrounded by death. Two aunts who had been living at Yasnaya Polyana died. In November 1874, the Tolstoy's youngest son died of the croup. Soon afterward came the death of an infant from meningitis, and subsequently Sofia had a miscarriage.

Tolstoy's acute obsession with death coincided with the writing of the last parts of *Anna Karenina*. While Anna dominates the novel, the book ends with Levin, because through Levin Tolstoy tries to control his own fear of death. But Levin is also important to Tolstoy for aesthetic reasons. He had grown too enamored of his heroine and, despite the punishments he visits on her, was not in control of his original purpose. Values could readily be drawn from the story different from the original motive—the punishment of an adulteress. However, the artist in Tolstoy, at war with the moralist, managed to free Anna from moralizing harassment "because the story of Levin and Kitty acted as a lightning-rod upon which the energies of didacticism were discharged." Without Levin,

"Tolstoy could not have portrayed Anna with such largesse" (Steiner 1959, 282–83).

Tolstoy the artist was in retreat because of his fear of death and his need to find a moral center. His wife's diary entry for 3 March 1877 suggests how important it was for him to believe in the idea of his novel. "Yesterday Lev Nikolaevich came to the table, pointed to a notebook of his writings and said: 'I'd like to finish this novel as soon, as soon as possible and start something new. I see my idea so clearly now. In order for a work to be good, one has to love its basic, fundamental idea. Thus, in *Anna Karenina* I love the *family idea*'" (Stenbock-Fermor 1975, 77).

By the sixth and seventh parts, in which the overwhelming number of pages are devoted to Levin and to characters surrounding him, the family idea had become the main idea of the novel. Tolstoy needed the evolving picture of the Levin family "as a large social unit (continuing the tradition of their forefathers) . . . from which radiates a creative, constructive force" (Stenbock-Fermor 1975, 84) as a corrective to Anna's passion. He needed to pour his own obsessive mood and thoughts into Levin in order to muster the energy to get through with the work, which, by the eighth part, resembles the author's diary.[13]

CONFESSION

It was as though I had lived a little, wandered a little, until I came to the precipice, and I clearly saw that there was nothing ahead except ruin. And there was no stopping, no turning back, no closing my eyes so I would not see that there was nothing ahead except the deception of life and of happiness and the reality of suffering and death, of complete annihilation. . . . However I may put the question of how I am to live, the answer is: according to the law of God. Is there anything real that will come of my life? Eternal torment or eternal happiness. What meaning is there which is not destroyed by death? Union with the infinite God, paradise. . . . Thus in addition to rational knowledge, which before had seemed to be the only knowledge, I was inevitably led to recognize a different type of knowledge, an irrational type, which all of humanity had: faith, which provides us with the possibility of living. (*Confession* 1983, 28, 60)

In April 1877, while Tolstoy was correcting the proofs for *Anna Karenina*, he wrote A. A. Fet that one absolutely has to think about God. At this time he began to attend church regularly, and he shut himself up morning and evening in his study to pray.

His book *Confession*, begun in 1879, describes his spiritual state and the thought process that led him to his own religious conclusions. At the heart is an account of his struggle to find philosophical relief from the despair of dying, which he conveys by way of an oriental fable about a traveler who is trapped in a dried-up well in the desert. He clings to a branch—a wild beast above him and a dragon below: "[W]hile he is clinging to the branch he looks up to see two mice, one black and one white, evenly working their way around the branch of the bush he is hanging from, gnawing on it. Soon the bush will give way and break off, and he will fall into the jaws of the dragon. The traveler sees this and knows that he will surely die. But while he is still hanging there he looks around and sees some drops of honey on the leaves of the bush, and he stretches out his tongue and licks them." Tolstoy continues: "Thus I cling to the branch of life, knowing that inevitably the dragon of death is waiting, ready to tear me to pieces; and I cannot understand why this torment has befallen me. I try to suck the honey that once consoled me, but the honey is no longer sweet. Day and night the black mouse and the white mouse gnaw at the branch to which I cling. . . . I see only the inescapable dragon and the mice, and I cannot turn my eyes from them" (*Confession* 1983, 30–31).

Science and philosophy could not provide the answer to the very thing that was leading him to suicide, "that life is meaningless" (34). To find stupefaction in sucking the honey was impossible, and yet, while suicide was always on his mind, he says that he was deterred by another "agonizing feeling. This feeling I can only describe as a search for God" (72).[14]

Tolstoy strove to accept the dogmas and rites of the Orthodox church, but much of it repelled him; fasts, adorations of relics, sacraments, church dogma seemed to him patent nonsense. "I want to understand, so that any instance of the incomprehensible occurs as a necessity of reason and not as an obligation to believe" (*Confession* 1983, 90–91). He could not stifle his relentless rationality; too much revolted him. He finally concluded: "I have no doubt that there is truth in the doctrine; but there also can be no doubt that it harbors a lie; and I must find the truth and the lie so I can tell them apart" (91).

His spiritual investigation resulted in a trilogy of books, which he came to regard as his most important works. *A Study of Dogmatic Theology* (1880) is a polemic against the teachings of the established Church. *A Harmony and Translation of the Four Gospels* (1883) is his most ambitious religious work; it demonstrates his thorough acquaintance with French, German, English, and Russian exegetical scholarship and his command of New Testament Greek. In this work he first formulates the five commandments that he believed encompassed the substance of Christ's original teaching, purified of the detritus of centuries of self-serving interpretations by the Church. *What I Believe* (1884) is the fullest exposition of his idiosyncratic version of Christianity up to this time. Simmons writes, "He approached Christ's teaching as a philosophical, moral, and social doctrine [and] firmly indicated his disbelief in personal resurrection and immortality. . . . The conclusion he reaches is that life is a misfortune for him who seeks only personal welfare which death in the end destroys, but a blessing for him who identified himself with the teaching of Christ and the task of establishing the Kingdom of God on earth, here and now" (Simmons 1968, 100).

Tolstoy dedicated himself to working for this earthly Kingdom of God. Believing that robbery and violence were implicit in ownership of property, he launched an all-out war against the aristocracy and against his wife and family. (He tried to divide his property among the peasants and wanted to give up the copyright to his writings. When his wife resisted, he gave all his property to her.) He did not instruct men to do good in order to achieve immortality but believed that to fulfill the commandments of Christ was to live in the Spirit, i.e., in a manner not subject to the annihilation of physiological death. Moreover, "[t]he theodicy of compensation, the belief that the tortured and the impoverished shall sit on the right of the Father in another kingdom, seemed to him a fraudulent and cruel legend calculated to preserve the existing social order. Justice must be achieved here and now" (Steiner 1959, 255). He attacked the Russian government for stifling and crushing essential human needs, and he condemned his own great artistic productions, and all of what is commonly regarded as literature, as specimens of class art: entertainment for the leisured and well-to-do class that imposes its will on the vast majority who do the rough work for them. After *Anna Karenina*, Tolstoy devoted the rest of his life to the propagation of his religious views.

POSTSCRIPT

The Marxists regard Tolstoy's anguish as a social rather than a moral phenomenon. V. I. Lenin wrote in 1911 that Tolstoy "recognizes only the standpoint of the 'eternal' principles of morality, the eternal truths of religion, failing to realize that this standpoint is merely the ideological reflection of the old ('turned upside down') order, the feudal order, the way of life of the Oriental peoples" (1963, 17:50).

Georg Lukács and Philip Rahv—whose reading of Tolstoy was based on Lukács—interpret Levin's agonizing overactive conscience in *Anna Karenina* as his way of resisting capitalism's ruinous triumph over the old order and, at the same time, as a rationalization for his right to own land and exploit his peasants. Pessimism caused Tolstoy to turn increasingly to religion in a futile struggle to find a way out of his dilemma. "His so-called conversion," Rahv says, "is the most dramatic and desperate episode in his stubborn and protracted struggle against alienation" (Gifford 1971, 236)—that is, in his fight to conquer pessimism and remain a landowner.

The Marxists look at Tolstoy's religiosity and appeals to the 'Spirit' in *Anna Karenina* as part of a historical presentation of his epoch. Turgenev, by contrast, was one of the first to lament the tragedy of Tolstoy's conversion.

I, for instance, am considered an artist ... but what am I compared with him? In contemporary European literature he has no equal. . . . But what is one to do with him? He has plunged headlong into another sphere: he has surrounded himself with Bibles and Gospels in all languages, and has written a whole heap of papers. He has a trunk full of these mystical ethics and of various pseudo-interpretations. He read me some of it, which I simply do not understand. . . . I told him, "That is not the real thing"; but he replied: "It is just the real thing." . . . Very probably he will give nothing more to literature, or if he reappears it will be with that trunk. (Gifford 1971, 224)

André Gide is contemptuous of Tolstoy's conversion. "What a monster! Constantly bucking, revolting against his nature, forcing one to doubt his sincerity at all times ... arrogant in renunciation, constantly arrogant, even to the point of not being reconciled to dying simply like everyone else" (Gifford 1971, 207).

But the world believed in Tolstoy's spiritual crisis, and the world regarded him as much more than a mere writer. Tolstoy became a religious sage after his conversion, and his texts on sex, death, purity, and corruption and his hunger for truth and salvation gave a moral force to his eminence unlike that of any man in his time except Gandhi.

A Reading

People are needed for the criticism of art who can show the pointlessness of looking for ideas in a work of art and can steadfastly guide readers through that endless labyrinth of connections which is the essence of art, and towards those laws that serve as the basis of these connections.

—Tolstoy's Letters, 1:297

5

Exits and Entrances: The Laws of the Novel

Stiva's Adultery □ Levin's Despair □ The Restaurant □ Anna's
Entrance □ Betrayal at the Ball □ Night Train to
Petersburg □ Anna's Homecoming

The Levin plot elaborates the truth of the aphorism with which Tolstoy
begins his novel: "Happy families are all alike; every unhappy family is unhappy in its own way" (1:1). There is one right way to live, one model for
happiness in marriage, and the Levin plot describes the conditions that
make it possible. What Levin achieves is natural, right, and good. If the
moral authority of the novel convinces the reader of this, Anna's tragedy
will be seen as proceeding from the second line of the novel on the track
of her brother's adultery.

Dolly has found out about Stiva's affair with their children's former
French governess, and he has been exiled from the conjugal bed: "Every
person in the house felt that there was no sense in their living together,
and that people who met by chance in any inn had more in common with
one another than they, the members of the Oblonsky family and household" (1:1). This is an exaggeration and works as a directive. One ought
to feel disgust for predicaments of this sort. The disruption to the children is inexcusable.

The description of Stiva's awakening is shrewdly accomplished: the
vigorous way he embraces his pillow; the silly amorous dream that he
ponders with a smile—"Yes, it was nice, very nice" (1:1)—the way he

cheerfully drops his feet feeling for his slippers; and only then the groan of recollection of "coming, happy and good-humored, from the theater, with a huge pear in his hand for his wife" (1:1) and finding her with the incriminating billet-doux in her hand; how, despite himself, owing to his indomitably healthy disposition, he had idiotically smiled. His dismay is nothing more than acquiescence; he is helpless to rectify what has been done, for to wipe away that idiotic smile he would have to convince Dolly that his infidelity has been an aberration and will never happen again. But Stiva has no intention of changing his ways. Anna's plump, pampered brother scarcely reproaches himself. He had thought that his wife guessed that he was occasionally straying "and shut her eyes to the fact. He had even supposed that she, a worn-out woman no longer young or good-looking, and in no way remarkable or interesting, merely a good mother, ought from a sense of fairness to take an indulgent view" (1:2).

Tolstoy is scathing in his clear psychological perception of Stiva, who rather congratulates himself on having been a good husband. Dolly, in his mind, ought to have no grievances. "I let her manage the children and the house just as she liked" (1:2). Furthermore, though it was vulgar of him to sleep with a servant of the house, was it his fault that she was so desirable? "But after all, while she was in the house I never took liberties" (1:2).

Tolstoy never eases up. Likable Stiva has been selling off his wife's property partly in order to finance his double life and feels deeply hurt by the thought not that he had been sacrificing his family to his double standard but that he might be prompted by self-interest to seek a reconciliation. His liberality with himself, Tolstoy submits, has made him a liberal in his political opinions and views—that is, a mild critic of existing institutions for reasons that have nothing to do with moral principles or political consciousness. Stiva is a liberal much in the same way that a person with a good digestion smiles contentedly after coffee and rolls. He is a liberal because he is clean and groomed and fragrant with eau de cologne and implacably healthy—feeling physically at ease in spite of his unhappiness. His good digestion makes him lusty, disgruntled with the restraints of traditional marriage, and restless in church. Hence, as liberals are prone to be, he is sympathetic to feminist views and is a nonbeliever.

Throughout the novel Tolstoy employs the same psychology for explaining his characters' behavior that he uses here to belittle Stiva and liberalism. Ideas and actions are merely the effect of bodily and material circumstances. Dolly wishes to be receptive to Stiva, but his glowing health and freshness affect her physically. She stiffens with hatred. And Stiva's tears and supplications evaporate the moment he leaves his wife, because of his irresistible resilience.

His colleagues find that they cannot help liking him. "His handsome, radiant figure, his sparkling eyes, black hair and eyebrows, and the white and red of his face" (1:5) unfailingly produce cheerfulness and pleasure. If asked to account for their delight in the man, each and all would commend him for his honesty; for, observing his lack of ambition (his work is never regarded as other than a sinecure) and the intense delight he took in dissipation, they considered that Stiva was a man to be trusted. He was, as his professional friends would put it, no hypocrite.

But honesty, to Tolstoy, means that, facing the fact of death, one must strip life to its essentials and not allow oneself to be deluded by its external trappings. The hero of the novel is driven by this desire for truth, and it has brought him close to despair. Levin is particularly ill at ease in the city; the decadent life of fashionable society, to which he belongs by birth, mortifies him with feelings of uncleanness and shame. Early in the winter, while courting Stiva's sister-in-law Kitty Shcherbatsky, the feelings of mortification (and the belief that he was physically ugly) had become unbearable, and he had left without proposing. But fear of a life without meaning has brought him back to Moscow; he sees dimly that marriage with Kitty will offer some kind of salvation. The theme of fear is announced during a debate that he overhears between two natural scientists at the home of his half-brother Koznyshev. Levin hears the scientists describing progressive, materialist beliefs, which are his own; but the scientists are untroubled by the conclusions to which their empirical interpretation of reality leads them. Levin too believes that consciousness derives from the conjunction of all one's sense perceptions, but this position seems to push him to a conclusion he cannot accept: "'If my senses are annihilated, if my body is dead, I can have no existence of any sort?' he queried" (1:7). The learned men ignore him. These concerns will later become obsessive. Koznyshev's intellect shields him from despair, but it also deadens him, making incandescent "sacramental" moments impossible. Levin, unlike Koznyshev, is haunted by the thought of their dying brother Nikolai, in whom he sees the spectre of himself, and this as yet unconscious dread lies behind his love for Kitty.

Kitty is very maidenly and chaste—"that little fair head, so lightly set on the shapely girlish shoulders, and so full of childish brightness and kindness" (1:9). Levin's rapture on seeing her has nothing to do with sexual desire. She awakens emotions in him that he identifies unconsciously with the innocence and religious faith of his childhood. The virginal bride in white represents Levin's hope of giving meaning to his life. He feels unworthy of her because he bears the stink of mortality, debauchery. The thought of his past experiences with women makes him appear revolting to himself. Levin fears that the finality of death will poison his will to live, and this underlies his dislike for the stupefactions of food and sex. It lies behind his prudery.

Levin's instincts are on the whole to be trusted, whether it is distaste for intellectual theories, contempt for office work, or revulsion for the painted French woman who is the hostess of the Anglia. "He made haste to move away from her, as from a dirty place" (1:10). Levin would genuinely prefer cabbage soup and kasha and chaste, girlish Kitty to the exotic cuisine and the decadence of Stiva's flashy existence, symbolized by the painted French woman with her ringlets. It is for her that Stiva is sacrificing his family, selling his wife's property, and stealing from his children, so that he can sit with "dewy, brilliant eyes" (1:10) in the Anglia eating oysters.

Levin experiences fashionable society as a Babylon. The decadence of luxury and debauchery, the titillation of nerves and the stupefaction it brings, disgust him because they smell of death. He becomes apprehensive about death the moment Stiva speaks of Vronsky, Levin's rival for Kitty's affections. "Very rich, handsome, great connections, an aide-de-camp . . . a cultivated man, too, and very intelligent" (1:11). Levin frowns, "[a]nd immediately he recollected his brother Nikolai and how loathsome he was to have been able to forget him" (1:11). Remembering Nikolai, he encounters again his own despair. Kitty stands for his hope in life; she moves him to feelings of rapturous reverence as well as profound unworthiness, and the mention of a rival accentuates these feelings.

Tolstoy shrewdly accomplishes the introduction of both his hero and heroine by beginning the novel with Stiva. The description of Stiva and his self-indulgent life enables Tolstoy to stage the entrance of his hero Levin and to point up by contrast his purer instincts. Stiva's adultery prefigures the story of his sister Anna. The similarity between brother and sister is underscored in the restaurant scene. Stiva says to Levin, "Before you've time to look around, you feel that you can't love your wife with love, however much you may esteem her." He goes on to confess that there are two women in his life. "[O]ne insists only on her rights, and those rights are your love, which you can't give her; and the other sacrifices everything for you and asks for nothing. What are you to do? How are you to act? There's a fearful tragedy in it" (1:11). Anna's story will make it impossible for the reader to agree with Levin's response: "I'm much obliged for the gratification, my humble respects"— that is, extricate yourself, since your duty is only to your family.

Chaste Kitty, with her "clear, truthful eyes" (1:13) likes Levin as though he were "a favorite brother" (1:9), sensing, perhaps, that Levin's feeling for her has no force of sexual desire. Tolstoy clearly approves; he attaches little importance to sexual attraction in determining marital suitability. Sexual attraction cannot be trusted—in Levin's mind lust and fear of death are linked inextricably—and society's view of sex is cynical. In the licentious atmosphere in which marriageable girls are hawked as if they were goods, Kitty rejects Levin for a dark, handsome, good-humored man with cropped black hair and "beautiful eyes" (1:14) —Count Aleksey Vronsky, who has been courting Kitty with no intention of marrying her.

Vronsky knows that Kitty loves him and is not troubled in the slightest by the fact that he is leading her on and spoiling her chances of other offers. She is a delightful novelty. That someone so sweet and tender should love him makes him feel "better, purer. I feel that I have a heart, and that there is a great deal of good in me. Those sweet loving eyes!" (1:16). And in a final flourish of egotism, he raises a silent tribute to Kitty for the spiritual regeneration she brings him and, temporarily ennobled, decides to pass up an evening at cards, drinking, and dancing.

By the time of Anna's entrance, Tolstoy has revealed the social and psychological tensions that coincide with licentious behavior. It is a strategy he never relaxes—an undercurrent of disapproval that works through his themes (the disruptions caused by Stiva's adultery, Levin's desire for purity, etc.) and through the artistic patterning of the chapters. Yet there is an equanimity in the narrator's tone and a brilliant reality in the continuous flow of life that transcends moral criticism. Despite Tolstoy's disapproval of illicit love, Anna's and Vronsky's encounter at the station is passionate and compelling. The scene is written from Vronsky's point of view. He cannot take his eyes off her. Shining gray eyes, the flash of a smile, the graceful quick step—this is all we see of Anna. Mainly we are impressed by an overbrimming vitality. Nabokov provides a composite portrait: "Anna was rather stout but her carriage was wonderfully graceful, her step singularly light. Her face was beautiful, fresh, and full of animation. She had curly black hair that was apt to come awry, and gray eyes glistening darkly in the shadow of thick lashes. Her glance could light up with an enchanting glow or assume a serious and woeful expression. Her unpainted lips were a vivid red. She had plump arms, slender wrists and tiny hands. Her handshake was vigorous, her motions rapid. Everything about her was elegant, charming and real" (1981, 227). But Tolstoy is already preparing Anna's tragic end. The crowd runs back onto the platform at the news of the accident, crying, "'What? . . . What? . . . Where? . . . Flung himself! . . . Crushed!'" (1:18). This is not accurate. Nobody flung himself. "A guard, either drunk or too much muffled up in the bitter frost, had not heard the train moving back, and had been crushed" (1:18). The mistaken idea of suicide anticipates later events. There is even a description of how the guard's wife "flung herself" upon the "mutilated corpse" in desperate grief (1:18)— just as Vronsky will later do. Shortly afterward in the carriage with her brother, Anna says, "It's an evil omen" (1:18), an expression that serves the unity of the novel and also shows Anna's profound fatalism. The words she next speaks questioning her brother about Vronsky imply that Vronsky is connected with her sensing an evil omen. Their lives are linked by a passion born under the shadow of tragedy. When Anna learns that the Shcherbatskys expect Vronsky to marry Kitty, her gesture indicates that she is deeply aware of Vronsky's appeal. She is described as "tossing her head, as though she would physically shake off something superfluous oppressing her" (1:18), and by that effort of will she tries to dispel the eerie apprehension caused by the encounter with Vronsky, the death at the station, and Vronsky's desire to impress her by his generosity to the widow.

Percy Lubbock, like Matthew Arnold, argues that Anna's immediate susceptibility to Vronsky is unintelligible. He claims (1921, 243–44) that there is no adequate preparation for it. "She has not yet become a presence familiar enough, and there is no means of gauging the force of the storm that is seen to shake her."

Lubbock would have preferred a Balzacian history of the Karenin household, and of Anna's past, and feels that the novel is flawed by the lack of it. He wouldn't deny that Anna has an unhappy love life. But Lubbock complains that we are given no advance evidence of her tempestuous passions and that she has already fallen into the trap of these passions before she is, in the reader's eyes, a fully realized human being. But it is precisely in the realization of her passions that she becomes, for us, a fully realized character. The crux of Lubbock's objection is that Tolstoy is writing like a poetic dramatist rather than a conventional realistic novelist and that the abruptness with which the reader meets Anna—the same abruptness with which the spectator encounters Lear—doesn't work for the novel. However, Tolstoy in his symbolically descriptive technique—the lidded eyes; the involuntary smile; the lock of hair that escapes Anna's otherwise perfect coiffure; the singularly light step—gives the reader an equivalent of the dramatic experience of actually seeing the character.

One thing is certain: there has probably never been a writer who has known as Tolstoy knows the reality of what he is depicting in its minutest detail. Dolly, whose point of view is always to be credited, tells us that there is something wrong with Anna's home life. She did not like what she saw of it when in Petersburg; "there was something artificial in the whole framework of their family life" (1:19). Kitty, infatuated with

Anna's youthful exuberance and beauty, observes "a serious and at times mournful look in her eyes," and this has her wondering about "the unromantic appearance of Aleksey Aleksandrovich, her husband" (1:20).

The reader requires no more than these few hints to be carried by the momentum of the narrative without resistance, believing, without as yet any deeper understanding, in Anna's struggle with the unsettling attraction she feels for Vronsky. She can scarcely suppress her passionate excitement. A luxuriantly sensual Anna emerges at the ball in a dramatic black gown with sumptuous lace, with a string of pearls, and with a spray of pansies in her hair. Anna with whom Kitty is infatuated and Vronsky from whom Kitty is expecting a proposal betray her without batting an eye; through her despairing gaze we see Vronsky with the submissive look of a guilty dog, and Anna bewitching and eager. There comes a moment at the ball when Anna and Kitty face each other. Anna, "with drooping eyelids" (1:23), presses Kitty's hand. This is the Oblonsky gesture of willful blindness to the consequences of immorality, and the family resemblance to the self-indulgent brother is meant to evoke distaste in the reader. But the big difference between the Oblonsky brother and sister is that Stiva has no conscience.

The continuation of Levin's story, immediately following the scene at the ball, begins with a self-reflection that would be equally valid for Anna. "'Yes, there is something in me repulsive and repellent,' thought Levin, as he came away from the Shcherbatskys' and walked in the direction of his brother's lodgings" (1:24). Levin finds himself repellent because his conscience accuses him of evasion and hypocrisy. Ultimately he will feel suicidal because he is incapable of spelling out honestly the demands of conscience and living by them. He compares himself with his brother, finding in Nikolai's reckless self-degradation and terror honest desperation. An atheist who had contracted tuberculosis, Nikolai has been living a life of dissipation and is now dying in squalor. In his brother, with those big "frightened eyes" (1:25), Levin, the uneasy unbeliever, sees a terrifying prophecy of his own end. Instinctively, he feels, after returning to his farm, that the answer to his agitation is in trying to be "better than before" (1:26). He must stop disparaging his work as a farmer, must stop "giv[ing] way to disgusting passion" (1:26). He must put himself more on a level with his peasants by working harder and reducing his few luxuries to the very minimum. He must also try to be a comfort to Nikolai. These are the resolutions of a man with a moral hangover, attempting to clear his conscience.

Anna makes a similar attempt to square herself with her conscience, but she fails to dismiss her flirtation as trivial. And yet, during the trip back to Petersburg, Tolstoy "celebrates" her "fall" into passion (Wasiolek 1978, 134). The word "celebrates" is appropriate, for despite Tolstoy's disapproval of her passion, the force of her personality is irresistible. She wants to live, but "there was no chance of doing anything" (1:29), and at the same time she wants to conquer her shameful craving for Vronsky. The violence of the snowstorm beating on the window, the shaking and rattling of the car, the rapid transition from steaming hot to cold—these obviously are metaphors for Anna's emotional turmoil. She feels a little hysterical and eerily dislocated from herself, as if out of control in a dream realm. "And what am I myself? Myself or some other woman?" (1:29).

In this delirium of rapture and fear, a figure appears whose role in Anna's destiny is like that of the blind, scrofulous beggar in Emma Bovary's—a "thin peasant who had come in wearing a long overcoat, with buttons missing from it" (1:29) and bends looking at the stove thermometer. Bursting with him into her dream state are terrifying images. "That peasant with the long waist seemed to be gnawing at something on the wall, the old lady began stretching her legs the whole length of the carriage and filling it with a black cloud; then there was a fearful shrieking and banging, as though someone was being torn to pieces; then there was a blinding dazzle of red fire before her eyes and a wall seemed to rise up and hide everything" (1:29).

These are surrealistic foreshadowings of her last moments. Her doom is embedded in her psyche, and she feels pleasurable dread in "sinking down" (1:29). Tolstoy etches into her unconscious the "sounds of a hammer upon iron" (1:30) just before she sees Vronsky and drinks in his confession of love. The symbolic language prepares her future: passion will tear through her life and destroy her. Anna feels panic-stricken but blissful.

The frigidly distinguished figure of Anna's husband makes a disagreeable impression on the reader, who first sees him through Anna's eyes. She notes, with dissatisfaction, the habitual sarcastic smile and the big tired eyes and is conscious for the first time of a long-standing feeling of physical revulsion for her husband. He has big ears and a prominent spine, he always adopts an ironic tone with Anna and lives a duty-driven existence. After meeting Anna at the station, he leaves her for a committee meeting, has dinner with her and their guests, attends another meeting, reads in his study, and goes up to bed punctually at midnight. Even on the night of his wife's homecoming, he cannot break out of his rigid schedule. Anna, her nerves frayed, attempts to restore a calmer judgment and return to married life. "'All the same, he's a good man; truthful, good-hearted, and remarkable in his own line,' Anna said to herself, going back to her room, as though she were defending him to someone who had attacked him and said that one could not love him" (1:33).

The one thing we feel consistently throughout the novel is that Tolstoy cannot plead a case against Anna, and the reason for this is simple: "The best books, the most full of infectious feeling, are those in which the author's intention is lost sight of, or even contradicted by, the close attention or 'love' which he devotes to his characters" (Bayley 1966, 241). This is certainly true of *Anna Karenina*.

6

Hounds and Mares: The Crime of Eros

Vronsky's Pursuit □ The Seduction Scene □ Hunting
Snipe □ The Steeplechase □ Varenka

Kitty, bitterly shamed and ill because of Vronsky's rejection, turns against her previous pleasures, angry at a marriage system in which her parents, by decking her out for eligible suitors, had made a kind of prostitute of her. She writhes from the doctor's examination as if he too were affronting her modesty. She feels sickened at the sight of her brother-in-law, Stiva, the epitome of lewd sex, and sees everything in the "coarsest, most loathsome light" (2:3). The man she had passionately loved had betrayed her; the man she might have married, whom she loved with "quiet affection" (1:9), she had refused.

Part 2 thus begins with an indirect indictment of passion. From the scene in which Kitty is sickened at having her modesty trampled, to the scenes of fashionable society where Betsy panders and Vronsky pursues Anna, an implicit link is being forged between Kitty, suffering humiliation, and Anna, being corrupted.

Vronsky feels no compunction about wooing a married woman. The affronted husband in the anecdote Vronsky tells Betsy has whiskers like sausages, because husbands whose wives are beautiful are buffoons to the dashing officers pursuing them. "He was very well aware that in their eyes the position of an unsuccessful lover of a girl, or of any woman free to marry, might be ridiculous. But the position of a man pursuing a married woman, and, regardless of everything, staking his life on drawing her into adultery, has something fine and grand about it, and can never be ridiculous" (2:4).

Naive eighteen-year-old Kitty does not understand the ways of the world—the way Betsy, after Vronsky leaves her opera box, lowers her bodice "so as to be properly naked as she moved forward toward the front of the box into the glare of the gaslight and the gaze of all eyes" (2:5). Anna is learning to make an immodest spectacle of love. "Anna walked into the drawing room. Holding herself extremely erect, as always, looking straight before her, and moving with her swift, resolute, and light step, which distinguished her from all other society women, she crossed the short space to her hostess, shook hands with her, smiled, and with the same smile looked around at Vronsky" (2:7). Yet that resolute step, which implies an emotional directness and honesty, is belied by the tone she adopts with Vronsky. She asks him to return to Moscow, to beg Kitty's forgiveness, and to marry her. This is patently insincere. Anna has limited herself exclusively to Betsy's social set in order to be accessible to Vronsky, and she finds herself replying to his passionate words with eyes full of love. This flirtation could not have occurred without the cooperation of fashionable society. Tolstoy condemns Anna's and Vronsky's behavior by prefacing their meeting with Kitty's humiliation, Vronsky's anecdote, and the scenes in Betsy's opera box and salon, thus demonstrating how the opulent world enables Anna's illicit passion to ripen.

The segment of chapters describing Karenin's jealousy is an elaborate composition, both verbally and psychologically. The formal, repeated register of his full name, "Aleksey Alexandrovich Karenin," and a series of picturesque similes evoke the pedantic rigidity and emotional impotence of the man. Karenin is afraid of moral difficulties; at the thought of stepping out of the worn groove of his life he experiences "a feeling akin to that of a man who, while calmly crossing a bridge over a precipice, should suddenly discover that the bridge is broken, and that there is a chasm below" (2:8). He insists on keeping up appearances, and he fears to confront Anna. "Like an ox with head bent, submissively, he awaited the blow of the ax which he felt was raised over him" (2:10). The rooms through which he paces correspond to his thoughts. He marches across the echoing parquet floor of the dining room (trying to compose a formal speech to Anna), through the carpeted drawing room with the big new portrait of himself (obsessed with his reputation), across Anna's lit boudoir to the bedroom door (shrinking away from the thought of her involvement with Vronsky), and back again to the lighted dining room (recalling the chamber in which Anna and Vronsky had sat tête-à-tête when he had entered Betsy's salon). Empathy terrifies him; he is appalled at the thought of Anna's having a separate life of her own. "'The question of her feelings, of what has passed and may be passing in her soul, that's not my affair; that's the affair of her conscience, and falls under the head of religion,' he said to himself, feeling consolation in the sense that he had found to which division of regulating principles his new circumstance could be properly referred" (2:8).

Self-absorbed and obsessed with his work—"[t]hinking over what he would say, he somewhat regretted that he should have to use his time and mental powers for domestic consumption with so little to show for it" (2:8)—he is a most unsympathetic character. Yet, perhaps drawing on some part of himself for this intimately detailed portrait of a repulsive pedant, Tolstoy occasionally makes him touching. Seeing that Anna doesn't care what he thinks, Karenin voices a genuine appeal. "Anna, is this you?" (2:9). But, on the verge of cuckolding him, she laughs at his appeal with dissimulated wonder. And so he delivers his prepared speech, a bad speech, implying that what is most disagreeable about her behavior is that it is causing gossip. Her rebuff throws him back on his guard, and he lapses into the habitual jeering tone that had been his way with her from the beginning of their marriage. It is the defensive posture of a lover afraid that his insecurity will render him vulnerable.

Anna's fall in 2:11 is described in language that presages the future of the two lovers, suggests their unconscious destructive urges, and conveys Tolstoy's ambivalence about passion and his intention to punish Anna. Her first reaction is guilt; Vronsky's is horror. Both feel shame. The language is brutal, the metaphors are of murder—his kisses hacking her body to pieces. "There is an unconscious will to murder in his sexual involvement, as Tolstoy shows in the images of sadism by which he describes their first love scene. And Anna is a preconsciously willing victim" (Cook 1967, 124).

Tolstoy foreshadows Anna's destiny, displaying from the start the moralistic animus he directs primarily against her, but also against Vronsky. She has no pleasure in this scene, no satisfaction. Feeling mortally wounded and horribly, shamefully exposed, Anna sinks to the floor and cannot raise her head. The prayer she addresses to Vronsky for forgiveness expresses her fear of being cut off from family and society and depending solely on him, a terrifying kind of solitude, which will eventually overwhelm and destroy her.

Levin, by contrast, having lost Kitty, has maintained a vow of chastity, unaware that his craving for spiritual peace is a yearning for the sustenance of his childhood faith. His vow of chastity is an effort to allay a pathological despair that threatens to poison his life. His theory of agriculture also derives from a need to have a clear conscience and be worthy of high justice. The chief point of the theory is that the science of farming in Russia has to take into account "a certain unalterable character of the laborer" (2:12). Levin is not to exploit his peasants for the sake of profit. Their communal life must be respected even if it means repudiating technological advances in agriculture from the time of Peter the Great. Levin proposes in his book to research the question of whether the agricultural technology of the West could have a place in Russia.

This segment, in which Tolstoy describes the coming of spring, and, more particularly, an evening of snipe hunting with Stiva, contains the sort of scenic painting that causes Turgenev, Mann, and Nabokov to assert that Tolstoy has no equal. "The place fixed on for the shooting was not far above a stream in a little aspen copse. On reaching the copse, Levin got out of the trap and led Oblonsky to a corner of a mossy, swampy glade, already quite free from snow" (2:15). One aspect of literary genius is this ability to enable the reader to see Levin leading Stiva from the trap to a particular spot swampy but largely bare of snow and to see Levin walk to a birch with a double trunk, lean his gun on a dead lower branch, remove his coat, fasten his belt, and begin working his arms, to make sure they are free. Even what the dog is doing (or more, what she is thinking) is of interest to Tolstoy. He describes the old gray dog sitting near Levin with her ears pricked warily, and the buds on the aspen trees "swollen almost to bursting" (2:15). With Virgilian power he heightens the reality of a spring scene (as with the later snipe hunt) and turns the natural into the sacramental: "The moon had lost all of its luster, and was like a white cloud in the sky. Not a single star could be seen. The sedge, silvery with dew before, now shone like gold. The stagnant pools were all like amber. The blue of the grass had changed to yellow-green. The marsh birds twittered and swarmed about the brook and upon the bushes that glittered with dew and cast long shadows" (6:12).

Lubbock says that "[d]aylight seems to well out of his page and to surround his characters as fast as he sketches them; the darkness lifts from their lives, their conditions, their outlying affairs, and leaves them under an open sky. In the whole of fiction no scene is so continually washed by the common air, free to us all, as the scene of Tolstoy" (1921, 44–45).

The segment ends by underscoring a chief theme of the novel's double plot: the contrast between the good and the depraved life. Levin fulminates against Ryabinin and Vronsky. Both represent the "progress" that means the death of the old aristocracy and the ruin of the life of nature. Ryabinin, like Lopakhin of Chekhov's *The Cherry Orchard*, belongs to a new class of rapacious merchants whose grasp is everywhere on landed property, turning forests into timber and ruining landowners. In his fury at Vronsky's claim of "blood," which ought to carry with it the responsibility of preserving the land, Levin turns nasty, attacking Vronsky's father, a man who "crawled up from nothing at all by intrigue" (2:17), and his mother, who slept with God knows whom. The crudity of his jealous remarks does not discredit the truth of what he says—that the agrarian gentry are the backbone of the nation; that he, Levin, and people like him, are the real aristocrats, who never curry favor, who value what they've earned by hard work, and who have moral fiber in their characters because they have principles by which to live.

When we last saw Vronsky and Anna, "[h]e stood before her, pale, his lower jaw quivering, and besought her to be calm" (2:11). Tolstoy achieves a remarkable transition in his return to the Anna story. "Although Vronsky's whole inner life was absorbed in his passion, his external life unalterably and inevitably followed along the old accustomed lines of his social and regimental ties and interests" (2:18).

With this opening statement, which darkens the narrative with its abruptness, Anna's tragic fate is announced again. Unlike Vronsky's, her external life will inevitably be changed: she will be excluded from polite society and deprived of her old interests. "'All is over,' she said; 'I have nothing but you. Remember that'" (2:11). Vronsky has begun to feel this pressure. Although well-connected, immensely wealthy, and brilliantly educated, he had been dallying in his regiment, playing the part of a kind of Prince Hal, who had assumed that "his lack of vulgar zeal" (Bayley 1966, 220) would commend itself to the people that mattered. But he has been passed over. He meets Anna, Bayley suggests, "when his role of disinterest [had] begun to pall" (220), and seeks to soothe his vanity by the notoriety of his liaison.

But ironically, his passion for Anna makes him refuse an opportunity "of great importance to his career" (2:18). Important people have become displeased with him. The day of the races he is repeatedly vexed by the voice of his thwarted ambition, and Vronsky's brother's displeasure states the attitude of fashionable society toward adulterous liaisons, namely, that Vronsky's affair wasn't frivolous enough, it annoyed the people who mattered, and therefore was indiscreet.

Tolstoy has strongly divided feelings about Vronsky. He finds it difficult to portray his strong points (after all, Anna has fallen in love with him) without at the same time disparaging him. The day of the races begins with his eating a beefsteak. This breakfast and his contempt for two homosexual officers are meant to impress us with his virility and self-possession. But his best friend in the regiment is a gambler, a drunkard, a person dangerous to have as an enemy, with a remarkable capacity for dissipation. Life for Vronsky, without the absorbing passion for Anna, is camaraderie with Captain Yashvin and horses; he is merely a "stallion in uniform" (Dostoyevsky in Knowles 1978, 288). Merejkowski writes, "If it is true that Vronski is like a horse in an aide-de-camp's uniform, then his mare is like a charming woman. . . . When he first looks at Anna he is struck by the 'race,' the 'blood' in her appearance. Frou-Frou too 'had in the highest degree this "blood," this "race"—a quality which made you forget all defects,' this aristocracy of the body. They have both, the mare and the woman, the same *definite expression* of bodily presence, which combines strength and tenderness, delicacy and energy. . . . They both have . . . the same over-stormy and passionate excess of vitality" (1902, 217–18).

Merejkowski's assertion that "Vronski loves the mare almost as a woman" (218) is persuasive. When Vronsky enters Frou-Frou's stall, she tries to nip him. "'Quiet, darling, quiet!' he said" (2:21), infected by her excitement and patting her on her hindquarters. "He felt that his heart was throbbing, and that he, too, like the mare, longed to move, to bite" (2:21). Tolstoy makes brilliant use of this symbolism later, in the segment when Vronsky breaks his mare's back and the portentous meaning of the steeplechase is horribly plain, with its indelible caption: "the crime of Eros" (Merejkowski 1902, 221).

Just prior to the lovers' meeting (which is the first we see of Anna since the fateful eleventh chapter), a powerful authorial interjection underscores the wrongness of their illicit passion. "This child [Anna's son Seryozha], with his innocent outlook upon life, was the compass that showed them the point to which they had departed from what they knew, but did not want to know" (2:22). Their passion is a misfortune causing mental strife for an eight-year-old boy. Anna appears in a white embroidered dress; she sits behind some flowers and presses her forehead against a cool watering can. Tolstoy's loving description of her hands, her movements, her hesitant disclosure to Vronsky that she is pregnant, shows most convincingly that the author is infatuated with his character.

Anna is terrified at the thought of Seryozha's future attitude toward her, and this terror paralyzes her. Why not have faith in the boy's ability to understand her? Why not have faith in her love for Vronsky and attempt a new life? Because of her legal position Anna knows that she is really stuck—if she tries to trust in Vronsky's love and try a new life it cannot include Seryozha.[15]

The accident at the steeplechase portrays, in some ways, the course their passion will take. Vronsky makes an unpardonable mistake in recovering his seat in the saddle and breaks Frou-Frou's back. "Again she struggled all over like a fish, and her shoulders setting the saddle heaving, she rose on her front legs, but unable to lift her back, she quivered all over and again fell on her side. With a face hideous with passion, his lower jaw trembling and his cheeks white, Vronsky kicked her with his heel in the stomach and again began tugging at the rein" (2:25).

This spectacle symbolizes Anna's fate, just as Tolstoy had foreshadowed it during Anna's postcoital scene in 2:11, where she feels murdered by Vronsky's passion and his jaw trembles. This, says Merejkowski, is what comes of passion, "that love which, full of hate—the thirst of physical possession akin to murder—finds expression in the most passionate endearments of lovers" (1902, 220).

In the remaining chapters of this section, the time shifts back in order to bring Anna to the races, where her panic at Vronsky's fall is described with the same imagery as is used for the writhing horse. Tolstoy oscillates dramatically between sympathy and antipathy for his heroine, making us despise her husband, then making her contemptible. Karenin suspects that his wife is an adultress, but he elects to avoid the truth, preferring to keep up appearances. He does not stay overnight at the villa because it might force a disclosure, and by coldly ignoring Anna he pretends to be punishing her for her aloofness. He meets his wife only once a week, and even then he always ensures that a third person is present.

But Anna, although pregnant with Vronsky's child, feigns pleasure at seeing her husband, pretending to want him to stay the night while burning with desire to be with her lover. Tolstoy probes the sources of her shame. Is this a fair portrait of a weak woman, or is Tolstoy using her to express his prejudice? Seryozha's "timid and bewildered eyes" (2:27) are a sign of the mental suffering his mother's misconduct is causing him. She is physically repelled by her husband, and that too, we are told, is shameful. But as she watches Karenin from her seat in the pavilion, we sympathize with her summary judgment of him. "'Nothing but ambition, nothing but the desire to get ahead, that's all there is in his soul,' she thought; 'as for these lofty ideals, love of culture, religion, they are only so many tools for advancing'" (2:28).

When Vronsky falls, Anna flutters like a shot bird. Nothing matters compared to her dread of her lover being dead. Repelled by Karenin's willingness in the carriage to hear and believe her lie, she tells him the truth he fears to hear. "'No, you were not mistaken,' she said deliberately, looking desperately into his cold face" (2:29). All judgment is suspended before the candor of the woman's blunt declaration. On the one hand, who could fail to sympathize with the injured husband? On the other, who would argue with her passion, with her feeling that a cold marriage cannot satisfy her instinct for life, and that to reconcile herself to Karenin would be false and deadly? "Perhaps Tolstoy himself believed that a loveless marriage for Anna was the better of two evils, and it is possible to draw this inference from the novel to provide a 'solution,' albeit an unhappy one. But so finely is the balance held that it is equally possible to draw many other inferences" (Christian 1969, 179).

The last segment of part 2 comments indirectly on the possibility of Anna's reconciliation with Karenin. In these chapters, Kitty looks to Varenka for "interest in life, a dignity in life" (2:30) apart from passion. She strives to emulate her, to learn "to disregard everything, to be calm independently of everything" (2:32) and to live for nothing but the good of her fellow creatures. Kitty yearns to be free of her longings, to live a more spiritual life, and she fantasizes a future in which she will seek out those in trouble, distribute gospels, and comfort the sick, the criminals, and the dying. This continues until the consumptive painter, Petrov, falls in love with her, and Tolstoy brings the old Prince Shcherbatsky to the German spa with his gusto, directness, and common sense. Her pretenses of independence and sanctity are exploded.

Varenka, with her feeble laughter, the silky hue of her face, her extreme thinness, and her overly large head, is not pretending to be other than what she is. She is drab, emotionally limp, and hardly likely to be attractive to men. She is at home in a "world of sorrow, of sick and dying people" (2:35). But naive Kitty, who scarcely has the passion of an Anna, soon finds her efforts to emulate Varenka intolerable, and part 2 ends with her "longing to get back quickly into the fresh air" (2:35).

If living with pretense is impossible for people like Kitty, it is hardly possible for Anna. The implication of the segment is perhaps this: for Anna to endure marriage to Karenin, she would have to sublimate her feelings like Varenka, turn "the heart into an institution: the situation so desired by Karenin, in which one no longer feels what one ignores" (Blackmur 1967, 135). This would be suicide.

7

Something Bitter Arises: Levin's Peasants and Anna's Passion

Levin Mowing □ Betsy's Croquet Party □ Vronsky's
Sacrifice □ Levin's Theory of Farming □ Nikolai's Visit

The opening segment of part 3 shows images of life overthrowing theory, that is, mowing wheat overthrowing social theories, as toward the end of the segment of chapters ending part 2, old Prince Shcherbatsky overthrows Kitty's idealization of Varenka. Levin is capable, as his half-brother is not, of a sensuous relationship with everything about him. Koznyshev is to be pitied for his self-absorbed existence. His philosophy and ideas of progress interest him in the same way as his chess problems and are equally remote from the real necessities of life. Thus, Levin, in the series of arguments with his brother, although apparently bested, is right and his brother is wrong—wrong, that is, to believe that whatever is foreign and comes from abroad is wonderful—progress, humanism, and traditional European culture. What is right is believing that the mainspring of personal and social action must be self-interest. Speaking in the author's voice Levin says, "why should I worry myself about establishing dispensaries which I shall never make use of, and schools to which I shall never send my children. . . . For me the district councils simply mean I have to pay eighteen kopeks for every three acres, to drive into town, sleep with bugs, and listen to all sorts of idiocy and loathsomeness, and self-interest offers me no inducement" (3:3).

The mowing scene in part 3 demonstrates that Levin, the landlord, is not an exploiter of peasants and is thus justified in his particular conception of agrarian paternalism. The more he loses himself in the rhythm of the work, the more he is in tactile relationship with everything about him. But the bliss he feels at these times lasts only so long as he does not force his will. When this happens, he is in a perfect frenzy of toil and incapable of looking about him. The peasant working the row in front of Levin never forces his will, and he therefore exists in a state of freedom that Levin can know only infrequently, when he is most at one with himself. The peasant, never once breaking the working rhythm, "picked a wild berry and ate it . . . looked at a quail's nest, from which the bird flew just under the scythe, or caught a snake that crossed his path and, lifting it on the scythe as though on a fork, showed it to Levin and threw it away" (3:5).

The language, conveying the sensuousness of the scene and the delight of the mowers, becomes lusher. "The grass cut with a juicy sound, and was at once laid in high, fragrant rows," and "they were continually cutting with their scythes the birch mushrooms, swollen fat in the succulent grass" (3:5). The surprising escape of Levin's persona from the lock-step rigidity of the work, his ascent from the field while still firmly present there, the light, the spaciousness of the scene, and Levin's joy convert the experience of mowing with the peasants into a sacramental moment.

Levin, vitalized by his experience, believes even more strongly that Western theories of agriculture—technological improvements, division of labor—will not only fail in Russia, but also destroy the social cohesiveness that is founded on the communal consciousness of the peasant class. Loosening this stabilizing bond—the inevitable effect of Koznyshev's progressive and enlightened theories—is a breach of faith with life that would lead to sterility and eventually to the rise of a proletarian peasantry dedicated to violence. Indeed, one can see in the mowing scene an illustration of the agrarian aristocrat's paternal ideal. Levin and his peasants act as one body. Obedience is not enforced. The primitive and natural order regulating the work comes from the nature of the task. The peasants and landowner are doing what circumstances necessitate. Moreover, by contrast to the peasants, whose communal life is glorified, the educated landowner, like Levin, acknowledges "a weary feeling of despondency at his own isolation, his physical inactivity, his alienation from this world," and longs "to exchange the dreary, artificial, idle, and individualistic life he was leading for this laborious, pure, and delightful life" (3:12). Although Levin cannot become a member of a peasant community, he can and must preserve the peasant's way of life, and his book on agriculture demonstrates to Russia, and to his own conscience, the necessity of doing this.

Tolstoy returns to Anna through Karenin, seated in his carriage the day of the races, "wrapping his numbed and bony legs in the fleecy blanket" (3:13) while passing in mental review over his options. The mind of the man, the phrases and logical constructions he uses in analyzing his moral difficulty, are an image of official bureaucracy. His thoughts proceed as through offices, hallways, and council rooms—calculating, cautious, and hypocritical—a sterile and inappropriate approach for coping with an emotional situation. When he finally decides to maintain the external status quo and warn Anna to cease all relations with her lover, Karenin piously observes to himself, "difficult as the task will be to me, I shall devote part of my energies to her reformation and salvation" (3:13). Tolstoy sneers at his stinginess and his opportunistic use of religious precepts; Karenin resents his wife's infidelity in part because it distracts him from his real life's work at the ministry. His letter warns her to be obedient to his wishes or lose her son, and having sent it, he throws himself with self-satisfaction into committee work. Tolstoy cannot resist describing at length this important work, which is important only to the bureaucrat and is costly and harmful to the nation. Such sustained authorial contempt for the husband, or perhaps the lies that he tells himself to deaden the pain and shame of his experience, tilts the reader's sympathy toward the adulterous wife.

When Anna appears, after an absence of twenty chapters, she is writhing with excruciating shame. She has not been able to tell Vronsky that Karenin knows of their affair, since that would be like proclaiming it to the world and forcing herself on him. Anna's end is again foreshadowed in her emotional state. She has no acceptable choices. She is not weighing her passion for Vronsky against the claims of duty. She is torn in two, and her psychological condition is dangerously unstable. On the verge of hysteria, she justifies her choice. "Haven't I tried, tried with all my strength, to find something to give meaning to my life? Haven't I struggled to love him, to love my son when I could not love my husband? But the time came when I knew that I couldn't cheat myself any longer, that I was alive, that I was not to blame, that God has made me so that I must love and live" (3:16).

Nevertheless, the puerile romanticism of this self-justification is probably designed to cheapen her as much as to convey her disturbed state. By the time Betsy's croquet party takes place, lying has become a positive source of satisfaction to her, even though it intensifies her feeling of guilt. Betsy's party illustrates the alternative to clandestine adultery. Liza Merkalova, with her entourage of lover and husband, is hardly an outcast. Sappho Stolz similarly makes a display of her lovers and belongs to the "cream of the cream of society" (3:17). Betsy advises Anna to look at things less tragically. Affairs can be handled; witness her lawn guests. But these women, exhibited by Betsy for Anna's edification, are speaking pictures of what fashionable adultery does to a woman. Sappho Stolz is a brazen tart; Liza, having become a concubine, complains of boredom and insomnia. Anna has the choice of continuing to lie or becoming like Sappho or Liza.

Anna, as yet, does not entertain the idea of emigrating with Vronsky, since emigration would be a crushing admission of her sin. Besides, "all around was that luxurious setting of idleness that she was used to" (3:17), and Tolstoy implies that she can no more imagine herself living outside this accustomed social atmosphere than can Liza, or for that matter Vronsky. Furthermore, to renounce that world would be to renounce her son and force Vronsky to renounce his career.

Critics on the whole have been hostile to Vronsky. He is too much the social animal. He interprets freedom only in terms of the social round. Wasiolek says that "in the depths of his feelings he is not much different from Stiva Oblonsky" (1978, 140), a superficial person with small passions. Christian, however, points out that Vronsky makes sacrifices for Anna's sake, though he is "[c]ommitted by birth and upbringing to the values and the way of life of a wealthy, conformist aristocracy, he renounces a brilliant career" (1969, 196), in order to remain in his regiment and accessible to Anna. To his credit, he resists Serpukhovskoy who, "smiling at him as tenderly as a woman" (3:21), offers him the highest professional advancement if he will abandon Anna. The offer doesn't tempt Vronsky. A note from Anna asking for a rendezvous leads him to gallop away from Serpukhovskoy and ambition.

The scene at the Wrede gardens is a trial of his love, and he acquits himself with credit. Anna knows in her heart that she will never have the strength to give up her position in society, abandoning her marriage to become his mistress. Forced to live and love in conditions she finds degrading, she wants to hear from Vronsky some "desperate, violent, decisive" (Wasiolek 1978, 143) declaration that will put an end to their false position. Just what he is to say she cannot imagine, but Vronsky must be her deus ex machina. At the rendezvous she gauges instantly the powerful effect she still has on him. However, he fails to show the appropriate zeal. He doesn't say, "Throw it all up and come live with me," and Anna becomes irritable and angry. "'For me there is one thing, and one thing only—your love. If that's mine, I feel so exalted, so strong, that nothing can be humiliating to me. I am proud of my position, because . . . proud of being . . . proud. . . .' She could not say what she was proud of. Tears of shame and despair choked her utterance" (3:22). These tears are not caused by any deficiency in Vronsky's love. This is the stranglehold of a drowning woman, and the scene shows his persevering tenderness for her in the face of her impossible demands.

Levin also feels forced to live a life he finds degrading. In order to make a livelihood, he has introduced agricultural improvements from the West, which the peasants rightly resist. Since he is convinced that their struggle is on behalf of "the natural order of things" (3:24) and against his profit motive, farming the land has become repugnant to him.

The big question for the landowner after the liberation of the serfs in 1861, "when everything has been turned upside down and is only just taking shape" (3:26), is what economic system to adopt with the emancipated laborer. But no system of farming appears to succeed. The reactionary feeling is that Russia has been ruined by the emancipation.

Liberals like Sviazhsky counter, "We must raise our farming to a higher level" (3:27). This means more of the kind of technological improvement that Levin cannot justify and that furthermore, he is convinced, won't work in Russia. Sviazhsky insists, "In Europe, a rational system succeeds because the people are educated; it follows that we must educate the people—that's all" (3:28). But to Levin this line of argument must be wrong because it leads logically to the destruction of "the natural order of things." Levin wants to believe that the landowner can adopt practices based on "the peculiarities and habits of our laborer" (3:27)—practices that satisfy the interests of both landowner and peasant while preserving the natural order, the patriarchal order. Hence, he disparages Sviazhsky. "You say schools, education, will give them fresh needs. So much the worse, since they won't be capable of satisfying them. And in what way a knowledge of addition and subtraction and the catechism is going to improve their material conditions, I never could make out" (3:28).

Levin's plan for solving the agrarian problem involves carefully preserving the peasant's values and traditions in order to repel revolutionary socialism. To repel it, while maintaining a patriarchal relationship between landowner and peasant as the basis of social order, "one must lower the standard of husbandry and interest the laborers in its success" (3:28). This is the core of his theory.

But progress, Marxist critics say, is a steamroller, and Levin's hope of minimizing his pangs of conscience is doomed. Since the only solution to the agrarian problem is to allow the peasants to manage their own lives, the conscientious landowner ought to divide his land among his peasants. Levin turns away from this stern counsel, depressed. Conversation at Sviazhsky's vitalizes his determination to solve his moral dilemma by "revolutionizing" his whole system of farming. But this can solve nothing, say Marxist critics like Bychkov, because the interests of peasants and landowners are diametrically opposed to one another; the fruitlessness of Levin's struggle with this social question "is the source of his deep pessimism" (1970, 828).

Through his theory, Levin is trying to reconcile his conscience with his privileges as a landowner. The theory also assures the peasantry the best of all possible lives. It is the only method of farming that can succeed in Russia, whereas scientific methods developed in the West always fail. And it entitles him to own his estate. Ownership, after all, which guarantees the peasants their old rooted place in the soil, is a sacred duty. The peasants imbibe their righteousness and their Orthodox faith from the land. Is he not then a defender of the faith?

But, of course, rationalizing his right to own the land does not give him peace; it sets him on the path toward an irreconcilable conflict. He cannot own the land (which involves exploitation) and hope to be worthy of eternal life. In this, as in much else, Levin is a surrogate for Tolstoy. Terror of death, and the emergence of a pronounced psychological need for the idea of God, put Tolstoy in the position of renouncing his attachments to the material world.

Levin's housekeeper, Agafya Mikhailovna, understands him in a way he does not understand himself. What lies behind his dream of "a bloodless revolution" (3:30) and general prosperity for the peasants? He says that he is doing it for his own good, meaning not for "the public good" and abstractions of that kind. This is true, but not in the sense he means. "'Of one's soul's salvation we all know and must think before all else,' she said with a sigh" (3:30).

His real motive becomes clear to him when he confronts the long, bony figure of his dying brother, "a skeleton covered by skin" (3:31), and recognizes in Nikolai a terrifying caricature of himself. "'Now I'm going to arrange my life quite differently,' [Nikolai] went on. . . . 'Besides, I want to turn over a new leaf completely now'" (3:31).

His brother's attempts to deceive himself horrify Levin because he also is trying to deceive himself. Nikolai's devastating attack on his theory of agriculture strips away his rationalizations, leaving him vulnerable to despair. "You don't want to organize anything; it's simply just as you've been all your life, that you want to be original, to show that you are not simply exploiting the peasants but have some idea in view. . . . [A]ll you want is to please your vanity" (3:32). Levin sets off on a foreign tour, obsessed with death and clinging to his agricultural scheme.

8

Forebodings and Transformations: The Divergence of the Twain

Nightmares ☐ Levin's Betrothal ☐ Deathbed Scene ☐ Karenin's Magnanimity ☐ Anna and Vronsky Elope

The inadequacy of earthly life is perhaps the theme of the novel. The despair that drives Levin to find his childhood faith by way of marriage to Kitty drives Anna to lose herself in carnal passion and finally in death. D. H. Lawrence chastises Tolstoy for rejecting a third possibility—sex as a life-giving force that is neither destructive nor sublimated into a spiritual ideal. Instead of seeking death or salvation, he says, Tolstoy should have revered the Anna–Vronsky relationship more than social law. But beneath Tolstoy's moral and social questions lies a deeper motivation, his fear of death, which made him obsessed with his own salvation. Lawrence, in criticizing Tolstoy for failing to celebrate freedom and a more abundant life for Anna, ignores the fact that she is not heroic to her creator. Rather, she exemplifies the futility of human nature, which destroys itself through passion that is fiercely attached to the material world.

The hero and heroine of the novel diverge in part 4. Levin sublimates the force of his discontented yearnings. Anna is consumed by her passion for Vronsky. The opening segment foreshadows her destructive end. Vronsky, seeing himself caricatured in the carnal excesses of a foreign prince ("'Brainless beef! Can I be like that?'" [4:1]), sinks exhausted into a dream identical to Anna's—a flash of telepathy, a bridge of nightmare linking them prophetically. Embedded in the psyches of both is the same filthy peasant with a disheveled beard. In Vronsky's dream he is "stooping down doing something" (4:2) and muttering incomprehensibly in French. In Anna's dream the small, dreadful-looking peasant is bending over a sack fumbling with his hands and talking rapidly in French: "the iron must be beaten, pound it, mold it" (4:3). In both dreams the dirty peasant is connected with carnal excesses and death.

The opening segment also contains a spectral image of Karenin, his face grotesquely like a death's head as he eyes Anna's lover entering his premises. "The gas jet threw its full light on the bloodless, sunken face under the black hat and on the white cravat, brilliant against the beaver of the coat. Karenin's fixed, dull eyes were fastened upon Vronsky's face" (4:2). All these are symbolic forebodings of death. Anna's passion, like Nikolai's consumption, is a relentless force that will destroy her lover and husband as well as herself.

Tolstoy oscillates between moral condemnation and love for his heroine, and the richness of the novel lies in the equilibrium he achieves between these contrary impulses, reflected in Anna's often repeated formula "guilty but not to blame." However, in the opening segment of part 4, Tolstoy shows more prejudice against his heroine than love for her. The progress of her deterioration has advanced considerably along with her pregnancy. She experiences embittered resentment and flashes of hatred for Vronsky—a jealousy of his freedom, his self-possession, his separate existence. To her this is infidelity, and her jealous fits have a chilling effect on Vronsky. "Both morally and physically she had changed for the worse. She had broadened out all over, and in her face at the time when she was speaking of the actress there was a malevolent expression of hatred that distorted it" (4:3).

Her mimicry of her husband, meant to entertain Vronsky, is too acrimonious to be amusing. "Could a man of any feeling live in the same house with his unfaithful wife? Could he talk to her, call her 'my dear'?" (4:3). What she says about her husband may be true, but Tolstoy is impatient and out of sympathy with her. He underscores her selfishness through Karenin's outburst: "What is base is to forsake husband and child for a lover, while you eat your husband's bread! . . . Yes, you only think of yourself! But the sufferings of a man who was your husband have no interest for you. You don't care that his whole life is ruined" (4:4).

Even though Karenin is mainly concerned with his reputation, he is so furious with Anna he is willing to initiate divorce proceedings, which are guaranteed to create a scandal. There was no civil authority that could grant a divorce in Russia until 1917. One had to appeal to the Synod of the Orthodox church, which could dissolve marriages on the grounds of adultery, either by proof (that is, detection of the fact) or by confession of either partner. The lawyer recommends that Karenin pretend to be the guilty party. But Karenin cannot adopt this method. Anna would sue him for divorce, would gain custody of Seryozha, and would thus deprive him of his power to hurt her. Frustrated but determined, he hires the lawyer as a detective to obtain details of Anna's adultery, preferring a sordid scandal to negotiating on her terms. The scene closes with the lawyer savoring Karenin's humiliation.

Throughout this opening segment of part 4, Tolstoy sounds dark chords of portents and premonitions. Levin's entrance is in this dark mood. His travels abroad, he tells Stiva, have convinced him that his solution to the agrarian problem is the right one. But he feels no excitement for the project; he is restless and depressed. Probed by Stiva, he says that he values his ideas and his work, but they signify nothing. "[A]ll this world of ours is nothing but a speck of mildew, which has grown up on a tiny planet. And for us to suppose we can have something great—ideas, work—it's all grains of sand. . . . So one goes on living, amusing oneself with hunting, with work—anything so as not to think of death!" (4:7).

The double plot has been moving to a crossroads, and at this point the lives of Tolstoy's hero and heroine diverge. Anna heads definitively toward suicide; Levin, deflecting his despair through marriage, moves toward faith in God. "Love cannot be exclusively carnal because then it is egotistic, and being egotistic it destroys instead of creating. . . . Tolstoy in a flow of extraordinary imagery depicts and places side by side, in vivid contrast, two loves: the carnal love of the Vronski–Anna couple . . . and on the other hand the authentic, Christian love, as Tolstoy termed it, of the Lyovin-Kitty couple" (Nabokov 1981, 147).

Blackmur states the contrast somewhat differently: "Human life cannot stand the intensity of Anna, but works toward it; human life requires the diminution of intensity into faith ... which is Levin" (1967, 145). Anna and Levin are alike in the intensity of their passionate natures. Anna's intensity can never find a fitting object, since no human being is large enough to receive it. She does all she can to make Vronsky as passionate as she is, but her craving to excite ever greater demonstrations of passion is inevitably thwarted. The only possible end for her is self-destruction. The contrast with Levin, whose love is not carnal, implies that it is not only Anna's circumstances that have caused her to become obsessed with death, but the nature of sexual passion itself. Levin conquers his despair because, in his worshipful love for Kitty and his gradual acceptance of religion, he redirects part of his passion onto an infinite object—God. Whereas the telepathy between the carnal lovers is a nightmare, Kitty and Levin's telepathy is chaste and delicate in the scene where they chalk initial letters on the green cloth of a card table (4:13).

Tolstoy's description of Levin's euphoria the morning of his formal betrothal to Kitty is reminiscent of those passages of Wordsworth in which the poet conveys the supersensuous mood of the adult as he comes into contact with his childhood. Unconsciously Levin associates marriage to Kitty with the religion of his childhood. Levin's compulsion to tell Kitty that he is not chaste and is a nonbeliever indicates his fundamental honesty. At some level of consciousness he feels vile and has no belief in the future. Kitty feels like salvation. Tolstoy accentuates her spiritual qualities by referring to the truthfulness of her eyes. The confession Levin makes to her by showing her his diaries chastens and humbles him. Carnal passion disgusts him because it accentuates his despair. It is physical, subject to decay and putrefaction; carnal passion is death. His confession to Kitty is his atonement. He wants her to see him naked in order to clarify his unworthiness and to bow down before her.

The debate over women's rights at Stiva's dinner party emphasizes the importance of the family and the central role of woman in it. It also discredits Anna. The narrative up to this point has established Dolly and Prince Shcherbatsky as trustworthy voices, while theorizers like Koznyshev and Pistov are untrustworthy ones. Since the argument that "[w]oman desires to have rights, to be independent, educated" (4.10) is anathema to Tolstoy, he speaks through Dolly. "If the story of such a girl were thoroughly sifted, you would find she had abandoned a family—her own or a sister's, where she might have found a woman's duties" (4:10).

This is more or less what Anna has done, and Karenin's pathetic condition has been in part caused by her. He has become an old broken man, his career at a dead end. The way he "cut off and spread with cheese a thin slice of bread fine as a cobweb" and rubbed "the tips of his fingers on his handkerchief" (4:9) conveys his enfeeblement. Anna gave coloring to his existence. His willingness to speak to Dolly before he commits himself in writing to the lawyer reveals his dejection. He is a very lonely, limp, cold fish.

Dolly's plea that Karenin not divorce Anna is based on her sense of social propriety. The hypocrisy of keeping up appearances, if it comes to that, is preferable to divorce. Karenin must be magnanimous. This is why she begs him, "Love them that hate you" (4:12).

Although Karenin would agree that magnanimity is desirable, it is fear of public opinion that brings him to Anna's bedside. "'And if it is true?' he said to himself. 'If it is true that in the moment of agony and nearness to death she is genuinely penitent, and I, taking it for a trick, refuse to go? That would not only be cruel, and everyone would blame me, but it would be stupid on my part'" (4:17).

Anna is so crushed by shame that she actually expects a blow from her husband when he walks into the bedroom. However, she gazes at him with "passionate and triumphant tenderness" (4:17). Through humiliation she has conquered her physical aversion for Karenin as well as her passion for Vronsky. This scene is unpleasantly melodramatic. Karenin, who in the past has always turned stony from agitation before another's naked emotion, ceases struggling with his feelings and sobs like a child. He gives his hand to Vronsky, compelled by Anna to pardon her lover. In a blissful spiritual condition, he pardons Anna as well.

Gorki's impression strikes me as valid here—that Tolstoy reveals his implacable hostility toward Anna. He pictures her as raving and writhing after her confinement, her pain and fever inseparable from her shame. The whole scene is demeaning to Anna; it shows the hostility, says Gorki, "of the male who has not succeeded in getting all the pleasure he could, or it is the hostility of spirit against 'the degrading impulses of the flesh'" (1920, 18–19).

Some critics read Karenin's emotional release as evidence that his forgiveness represents genuine love. He says to Vronsky, "you can trample me in the mud, make me the laughingstock of the world, I will not abandon her, and I will never utter a word of reproach to you" (4:17). Probably it is this lofty resolve that convinces Stenbock-Fermor that all along Karenin was a sincerely religious person who had "genuinely believed that keeping his wife and pretending that all was well was not hypocrisy, but magnanimity, as it saved Anna from social ostracism" (1975, 93). But there is far more evidence that just the opposite is true; all Karenin's past behavior conflicts with this interpretation and shows him to be an opportunist in religious matters. Nevertheless, Vronsky sees that Karenin's behavior now is "not false or ludicrous, but kind and straightforward and dignified" (4:18), although it inspires in Anna, predictably, physical revulsion and hatred.

Tolstoy blames social opinion—that "brutal force" (4:19)—for the revival of Anna's physical repugnance. The epitome of this force, Betsy, browbeats Anna to see Vronsky. She has pandered for Vronsky, and when Anna elopes with him, Betsy, who has brought them together and who feels contempt for Karenin, will refuse to invite Anna to her home. In other words, Tolstoy is saying Karenin is noble, society is despicable. The idea of Karenin doing something definitive is discredited by coming from the mouth of Betsy while she is flirting with Stiva. "One of two things: either let him take her away, act with energy, or give her a divorce. This is stifling her" (4:21). Nevertheless this strikes us as true, as does Anna's dilemma, which Anna describes, "Would you believe it, that knowing he's a good man, a splendid man, that I'm not worth his little finger, still I hate him. I hate him for his generosity" (4:21). Karenin's aversion to divorce is spoken in the author's voice; he says that Stiva's appeal to divorce Anna is wrong. The authorial position is that marriage was "the last prop that supported her on the path of virtue" (4:22). Anna's ruin is foreshadowed by Vronsky's attempted suicide as a way of coping with the humiliation of being cast out. Vronsky lives by a code that demands that he shoot himself because Karenin has made him appear ridiculous. By this act, Tolstoy says, "he had, as it were, washed away the shame and humiliation he had felt before" (4:23). Vronsky is denoted by his powerful square jaw, strong teeth, and hairy chest. He draws his strength from the solid ground of his code as Antaeus does from the earth. His honor is restored by the desperate act. He can lift his head and be accepted among his peers, whereas Anna will collapse under the malice of society.

Society, through its symbolic representatives Stiva and Betsy, pressures Karenin into agreeing to a divorce. Vronsky flies to Anna, and she, turning pale as death, "getting whiter and whiter" (4:23), surrenders to her passion for him.

Anna refuses Karenin's generous terms for a divorce, including custody of her son, because she cannot tolerate the thought of being beholden to him. At the same time, she understands that right behavior and reform in marriage with Karenin have been offered her and that by rejecting it she is turning her back on all social conventions—giving up all for love. Her recklessness is an unconscious will to self-destruction. "She begins to be touched by the momentum and menace of her own doom" (Thorlby 1987, 81).

While it is true that from an artistic point of view Anna must neither become reconciled to Karenin nor find a path of acceptable escape from him, Tolstoy's equivocal attitude at the end of part 4 does not seem to be in his artistic control. From the deathbed scene onward he tries to convince the reader, and himself, that, had society not interfered, Anna would ultimately have become reconciled to Karenin.

To many readers including D. H. Lawrence, Anna, not Levin, is the moral exemplum of the novel. Her struggle for emotional honesty and freedom against the constraints of social convention also claims the admiration of R. P. Blackmur. He sees in it an example of moral courage, tragic because heroic stories like Anna's are always tragedies. Had she not boldly attempted her new life, he says, "there would have been nothing to break down, only the collapse of a dry shell" (1967, 139). In short, her cause is good although her strength is not sufficient.

Readers will naturally mute and amplify the mixed evidence of Anna's story according to their predilections. The ambiguity of life itself makes up the richness and mystery of this greatest of Tolstoy's characters.

9

Wives and Mistresses:
Love against Death

Levin's Wedding □ Italy and Mikhailov □ Nikolai's
Death □ Karenin and the Countess Lydia □ Anna
Visits Her Son □ The Opera

Levin's story is Anna's counterpoint. The four segments of part 5 are arranged to demonstrate the contrast between lawful Christian love, which
deepens into mutual respect, and the bitter ecstasy of illicit passion,
which turns to jealousy and hate. Levin and Kitty are solemnly conse-
crated to one another during the opening sequence throughout which
the very completeness of the ceremony, in all its tender and bewildering
aspects, reminds us of the opposite in Anna and her connection to
Vronsky. The priest's probing of Levin's avowed atheism makes him
vaguely conscious of "something not clear and not clean in his soul"
(5:1), and like Anna he evades it. His pang of conscience gives rise to a
sudden terror that Kitty doesn't and can't love him, and this terror will
be amplified and darkened in the story of Anna who has, in fact, been
false to her conscience and will be destroyed by it. Kitty, too, is Anna's
opposite. "She could not frame a thought, not a wish apart from life with
this man" (5:4). The readings in the ceremony also present Tolstoy's ide-
alistic view of marriage: "from Thee woman was given to man to be a
helpmeet to him, and for the procreation of children" (5:4). By implication Tolstoy indicts Anna who has broken the law of woman's nature,
which is to be fruitful and obedient. Her failure is underscored by

Levin's success. Dolly, moved to tears by Kitty's joy, thinks "too of her darling Anna, of whose proposed divorce she had just been hearing. And she had stood just as innocent in orange flowers and bridal veil. And now?" (5:5).

In Italy Anna is temporarily reborn, but her transient happiness is marked by omens of disaster. She is afraid of not behaving as Vronsky wishes. Yet her abject dependency on him is not humiliating to her. Since she has just been freed from the tomb, nothing poisons her mood. She secretly acknowledges an almost slavish adoration of Vronsky. In Italy her dependency satisfies her; she is content possessing him. In Russia that same passion becomes vicious.

The Mikhailov episode answers the question, why couldn't they live as expatriates forging a new existence for themselves? The simple, immediate answer is that Vronsky needs work—or at least distraction. Whereas in Russia, as a cavalry officer and a man of society, he had never lacked for things to do, here, being idle, he takes up painting and discovers that he has a pretty talent for imitation. But this is mere dilettantism, which can have no hold on a man of energy, and it is thrown into perspective by the artist Mikhailov. Mikhailov's intense fervor excludes all other interests. Art is the sternest of mistresses. He is irascible as well as obsessive about his work and pathologically sensitive to criticism. Anna could not have tolerated Vronsky had he possessed the real gift, and Vronsky cannot make a career out of being merely a dilettante and a lover.

Mikhailov, who precipitates the end of their honeymoon, shows them his masterpiece—Pilate sentencing Jesus to death (5:12). Both miss Mikhailov's supreme achievement, the look on John's face. Anna and Vronsky turn away to admire the physical beauty of two young boys angling by a summer pool. Tolstoy implies that Anna should turn from this summer idyll and take up her cross—turn back, that is, from the folly of ephemeral passion, self-deception, and death, to duty, faith, and the joyful serenity that is virtue's reward. Yet it is also possible to read the symbolic import of the painting in another way: not that Anna is wrong in refusing to accept the cross of a loveless marriage to Karenin, but that society is wrong to judge her; the picture represents not a moral warning, but a foreshadowing of the tragic death of a person who is good, innocent, and admirable. Critics have often found it hard to distinguish which strand of the many in Tolstoy's hand is being examined at any given moment. All of Tolstoy is a battle between his feeling for complexity and his hunger for simplicity. In Berlin's view this tension is the source of Tolstoy's creative power.

The foreign idyll ends when Vronsky, confronted by the superior genius of Mikhailov's portrait of Anna, gives up painting, and the couple decides to return to Russia. There can be no other world for these lovers but the cliquish, fashionable set to which Vronsky diverts much of the current of his life and from which Anna is excluded.

The Levin-Kitty relationship is also troubled in one essentially similar way. Levin feels that love is cloying, and he is growing restless. Disconsolate about his inability to work and irritated by the thought of being under Kitty's thumb as well as by fear that she is bored with him, he begins talking to himself: "I ought myself to be firmer, to maintain my masculine independence" (5:15). He has no self-possession when she is angry with him. His sense of well-being is too dependent on her moods. Moreover, he thinks her frivolous: "she has no serious interests. No interest in her work, in the estate, in the peasants, nor in music, though she's rather good at it, nor in reading. She does nothing, and is perfectly satisfied" (5:15).

Tolstoy, however, intrudes here to tell us what Levin does not understand—that Kitty's real work lies ahead in being the mother of his children—and the strategy of the segment is to open Levin's and the reader's eyes to the significance of this fact. For this reason, the incident of Nikolai's death is skillfully placed during the early, troubled period of their marriage.

Nikolai's hideous struggle with death externalizes Levin's worst fears. "The utter futility, the crude physical horror, even obscenity, of the scene are almost intolerable" (Christian 1969, 181). Levin can do nothing for his brother but exasperate him. He cannot hide his horror, which conveys the message: die, for you're as good as dead, and nothing can be done to relieve your suffering. Kitty demonstrates what women can do and men can't: relieve suffering. The secret of Kitty's, and Dolly's and

Agafya Mikhailovna's, ability is a belief in miraculous cures. Kitty is able to infuse hope into Nikolai because she acts in accordance with her belief that miracles are possible. Thus, she can work to make her patient comfortable and can concern herself with his condition. Behind this marvelous healing gift of women lies an instinctive faith in the greater miracle to come. This too Kitty imparts to Nikolai—the quieter hope of a better life after death.

For ten days Levin watches his brother wrestle with death, and yet he does not despair, although he sees enacted before him the truth he feared would drive him to suicide. Kitty illustrates the reality of faith, which Mikhailov revealed in the expression on John's face and which Levin now implicitly acknowledges. Burgeoning faith saves him from despair and makes his love for Kitty "stronger and purer" (5:20). The segment ends with Kitty's pregnancy, completing the image of a virtuous woman, whose husband and children will rise up to praise her.

Anna, in the final segment, returns to Petersburg and reality. Her entrance is preceded by an elaborate preparatory scene. At this point in the novel Karenin is a pathetic, lonely man needed by no one and rather despised for the oddity of his behavior to Anna. The solace that the Countess Lydia Ivanovna rushes to offer him is a caricature of Christian charity. Tolstoy can't resist parodying the message implicit in Mikhailov's painting and Kitty's nursing of Nikolai; he doesn't quite believe in his hero's impending salvation and can't disparage passion, either. Karenin gazes into Lydia's beautiful, dreamy, compassionate eyes and tells her that he feels "crushed . . . annihilated," and that he's "no longer a man" (5:22). She tells him, "Our support is love, that love that He has vouchsafed us. . . . He will be your support and your succor" (5:22).

But the Countess Lydia is a little too ecstatic; Karenin cracks the joints of his fingers. And then the veil of sanctity is altogether rent when Lydia, after praying and lifting her eyes heavenward, marches into Seryozha's part of the house, "and dropping tears on the scared child's cheeks, . . . told him that his father was a saint and his mother was dead" (5:22). Karenin clings "to his mock salvation as if it were genuine" (5:22); he needs it as a crutch in order to walk about. Tolstoy continues to belittle Lydia with venomous irony. Her attack of asthma from excitement on receiving Anna's letter, scented with "delicious perfume" (5:23), is wonderful satire. This paragon of Christian compassion has enough vindictiveness in her for two.

Karenin would not prevent his wife from seeing her son. But this does not sway Lydia's jealous hatred of Anna. But Karenin's cruelty to Anna is not so much a result of Lydia's vindictiveness as that "brutal force," social opinion, which makes him shrink from playing the fool again. The genuine emotion that had overflowed when he forgave his wife had ultimately made him ridiculous. He has become the prey of his own self-derision, tortured by the thought that he hadn't challenged Vronsky to a duel, that he had forgiven Anna, and that he had actually been prepared to love her bastard daughter. This internalizing of society's judgment is at the root of his capitulation to Lydia. He is not about to invite its mockery a second time by playing the well-meaning, impotent cuckold. A fear of sexual impotence causes him to recall his awkward hesitancy when proposing marriage to Anna, and then to visualize with hatred "a whole series of those juicy, vigorous, self-confident men, who always and everywhere drew his inquisitive attention in spite of himself" (5:25).

Anna is mortified by the insulting reply from Lydia. When Karenin comes upon her in Seryozha's room, bowing his head helplessly and turning his other cheek, she is prey to violent oscillations between a crushing sense of shame and fury. At the same time, the fervor of her feelings for her son, her admiration for his fresh, sensitive, inquisitive nature, and his and the old house servant's love of her convey the vitality and beauty of the woman.

Humiliated by the shame of her position, she rushes back to her hotel rooms longing for Vronsky's love and dresses carefully, anxious to please him. She requires his exclusive and impassioned attention, but he is occupied with Yashvin, talking about horses. Bitter that she has abandoned everything for him and is even hiding her thoughts to protect him, she is further outraged that Vronsky is busy with his friend and impatient to leave her. Everything conspires to wrong her—Countess Lydia's malice and hypocrisy, Betsy's hypocrisy, and now Vronsky's betrayal. He has been colder, both because his love has been strained by the chilling recep-

tion Petersburg society has shown Anna and because her behavior is trying his love. She fears that his love is dying, and her fear expresses itself in
possessiveness. Hence he grows aloof, and this aloofness confirms her
fear and turns it into hatred of him. Part of her wants to hurt him, part of
her wants to assert herself; attending the opera is a way of doing both.
Wounded by his indifference and inflamed by the world's scorn, she
turns to ever more defiant behavior. Attending the opera is social suicide,
a way of being punished as well as punishing; it may also be Anna's way of
gaining control of her life. Whether driven to destructive behavior by
conscience, by a desire for independence, or in fulfillment of a death
wish, Anna gradually poisons Vronsky's love of her.

From the stalls in the opera Vronsky scans the boxes of the forty or
so *"real* people" (5:33) (how few compose her world), readily discerning
from their eyes the position of Anna's box. He notices how beautiful she
is and is reminded of her at the ball in Moscow. "But he felt utterly different toward her beauty now. In his feeling for her now there was no element of mystery, and so her beauty, though it attracted him even more
intensely than before, now offended him too" (5:33). Her beauty does
not protect her from the insults of society either. The Katavasovs vacate
the box next to her as if she were infected. "Anyone who did not know
her and her circle, who had not heard all the utterances of the women expressive of commiseration, indignation, and amazement that she should
show herself in society, and show herself so conspicuously with her lace
and her beauty, would have admired the serenity and loveliness of this
woman without a suspicion that she was undergoing the sensations of
someone in the stocks" (5:33).

Freudian critics have speculated that Anna exemplifies something in
the human condition that seeks death. Judith Armstrong says that
Vronsky and Anna's passion is sadomasochistic, sadism and masochism
being concomitants of narcissistic love, which is particularly strong in
their affair because of "their unfamilial childhoods" (1988, 98). Their
first love scene, she says, has "all the elements of rape," as Vronsky's aim
throughout "is clearly to master Anna" (89). Anna's masochism increasingly expresses itself as anxiety that she is not loved. She "persists in
calling forth her anxiety—that is, in provoking Vronsky to anger or

irritation, which she then experiences as the cessation of his love" (103). This anxiety, Armstrong says, quoting Harold Bloom from another context, is "'anxiety determined to go on being anxious, a drive towards destruction, in love with the image of self-destruction'" (103–4).[16] It also appears obvious that Anna blocks her own happiness by creating obstacles to it and that a motive to her attending the opera may be to create a barrier to her satisfaction in order to "swell the tide of libido to its height" (72).[17] Death is the ultimate obstacle, and death is the aim of passion from the beginning. Thus, based on these psychoanalytic speculations, one might say that Anna attends the opera because unaware, and in spite of herself, her love has had only one object—the desire for death.

10

Something Bitter Arises: The Inadequacy of Earthly Life

Levin's Jealousy ☐ Debate with Stiva ☐ Dolly's Visit ☐ Anna's Desperation ☐ The Provincial Elections

> A spiritual forgetfulness co-existed with an intellectual remembrance. She walked in brightness, but she knew that in the background those shapes of darkness were always spread. They might be receding, or they might be approaching, one or the other, a little every day.
> —Thomas Hardy, *Tess of the d'Urbervilles*

Levin and Anna are contrasted in part 6 as divided selves, each holding tight to a surface tranquility. Levin is busy doing good, running about from one duty to another, tending his guests and the estate, while thinking: "I envy him [Koznyshev] for being better than me. . . . He does not live for himself. His whole life is subordinated to his duty. And that's why he can be calm and contented" (6:3). Levin cannot be calm and contented, not because Koznyshev is better than he, but because he has been evading the chief issue of life—how to live in face of death.

The touching, faintly pathetic romance between Sergey Ivanovitch Koznyshev and Varenka (a short-short story complete in itself) expresses Tolstoy's awareness of the power of the unconscious and the corresponding impotence of the will. In spite of good intentions and reasonable desires, the deepest urges govern one's actions. The pious Varenka and the aging intellectual walk through the wood intending to talk about marriage, but the moment slips by, and instead of marriage they discuss the difference between birch mushrooms and white mushrooms.

Despite his happiness, which is the coda to this little scene, Levin cannot resist the pressure of his suppressed fear of death. It breaks forth, although in a preposterous disguise. "Already he saw himself a deceived husband, looked upon by his wife and her lover as simply necessary to provide them with the conveniences and pleasures of life" (6:7).

His jealousy of the "stout young man in a Scotch cap, with long ribbons behind" (6:6) is extreme and ludicrous. But one remembers what attracts Levin to Kitty. She is "family" to him—the replacement of the family he never had and the author of the family to come. It is significant that he had looked to the Shcherbatskys as a surrogate family and had courted Kitty's two older sisters before her. She is connected with his childhood in yet another sense—one might call it Wordsworthian rapture, a coming in touch with the "dearest freshness" (Hopkins) of his own nature in the sacredness of his feelings for her. She is his better self. There is nothing lewd in his feelings for her. She is, in a mysterious way, his bid for salvation, his means of defeating the despair to which he is susceptible. The lewd, sensually corrupt Veslovsky with his fat calves and ribbons desecrates Kitty with his attentions, whereas Levin limits himself to kissing Kitty's lips and hand; we never see him desiring her. His jealousy expresses exasperation with Kitty for not taking the burden of his salvation on her shoulders, for not being a complete safeguard against his fear of death. Eventually Levin honestly confronts the dilemma of a man of science needing God and makes a choice. By placing his hope of salvation in God rather than in Kitty he liberates her. But Levin in part 6 is still seeking stopgap measures against despair. He worries that he is merely shilly-shallying with his conscience in the work he is doing on behalf of his peasants. Can a landowner not be an exploiter?

His dissatisfaction with himself arises again during the snipe hunt, which is a shaggy-dog story designed to play upon his nerves and provoke a confrontation with Stiva. Veslovsky is a caricature of Stiva. Both are hedonistic and self-absorbed. After the long day's frustration, Levin, in a bad temper, aims a barb at Stiva's crude hedonism. But he goes about it indirectly and lays himself open to attack in the process. "[A]ll profit that is out of proportion to the labor expended is dishonest" (6:11), he says, and he goes on to attack banking, railroad companies, and liquor companies as sinecures for people like Stiva to make money without work. Behind his attack is also his theory, which exonerates him from blame for the impoverishment of Russia. The anomalous distribution of landed property is not the cause of the disastrous condition of agriculture; this disaster arises from centralization of industry in towns and the resulting decadence which arises from an increase in leisure (5:15). Stiva calls him a hypocrite and attacks him for not rectifying the injustices on his own estate. He tells Levin one must "either admit that the existing order of society is just, and then stick up for one's rights in it; or acknowledge that you are enjoying unjust privileges, as I do, and then enjoy them and get all the pleasure you can out of them." Levin's answer clarifies just how far he has gone. "The important thing for me is to feel that I'm not guilty" (6:11).

This is hardly a fortified position. Levin has a way to go yet in his journey to faith, and the segment closes with an amusing illustration of this very point. Once more he accuses Kitty of flirting with Veslovsky. His jealousy, however, is a psychological pretext. He digs in his heels and bellows his disappointment with Kitty. This irrational breaking out is a beginning, a psychological crumbling that will eventually lead to his crisis of faith. Anna similarly would compel Vronsky to relieve her of despair, to be her salvation, but will resort more frequently to cordials of wine mixed with opium. Things are simpler at Levin's country estate, where the fancies of a bad conscience tend toward farce rather than tragic opera.

Dolly comes to Anna, admiring and envious of Anna's courage to risk everything for love. Anna gallops to the carriage and springs from her horse, the romantic heroine whose radiant beauty dazzles Dolly. But Anna's "little court" (6:19) consists of sponges and castaways—Princess Varvara and Veslovsky, and Betsy's ex-lover Tushkevich. Only gradually is Dolly disturbed and finally shocked by Anna's condition.

The baby's nursery is large, light, and airy. That is good and to Anna's credit. But everything is imported from England and extremely expensive—"appliances for teaching babies to walk, and a sofa after the fashion of a billiard table, purposely constructed for crawling" (6:19). The baby has a Russian nursemaid, an English head nurse (a disreputable-looking woman), and a wet nurse whose milk is dried up. Dolly sees at a glance that Anna has very little to do with her daughter, and Anna confesses to feeling "superfluous" in the nursery (6:19). This belies Anna's insistence that here she is "perfectly at ease and happy" (6:19).

At dinner Dolly realizes that Anna has no responsibility for the management of the house. Anna is playing hostess. She is, in fact, as much Vronsky's guest as is Veslovsky. But most evil-smelling is the tension that Dolly perceives at the table. Vronsky wants to make a life out of being the country squire, but Anna resents any activity that takes him away from her. He wants to believe in his work; Anna wants to believe in his love. He demands freedom to come and go; Anna insists that he put an end to her misery.

Finally Anna and Dolly have their long promised and long delayed tête-à-tête, at which Anna reveals her state of mind. She tells Dolly that she is repelled by the thought of suing for a divorce. She hates the hypocrisy of fashionable society and will make no concessions to it. And then she adds gloomily, "What wife, what slave can be so utterly a slave as I, in my position?" (6:23). What she has done is irreparable; only Vronsky's passion makes life worth living. Legalization of their relationship is not important to her. She shuns the thought of a divorce because it would give Vronsky the freedom to pursue his political ambitions. "In effect, Anna would end up being tied to another Karenin, a possibility signaled by the fact that both men have the same first name" (Wasiolek 1978, 142).

To the argument that a divorce will enable her children with Vronsky to be Vronskys and not legally Karenins, she answers that she will never again disfigure herself with pregnancies. From Tolstoy's point of view—and this is emphasized by Dolly's appalled and astonished reaction to the news that Anna is practicing birth control—Anna's circumstances condemn her to sterility. Everything about her life is unnatural. It consists of entertainments and distractions—a game of tennis, a row on the lake, evening tea. She has no work and can have no work without children, and she can have no more children because she must remain attractive to Vronsky. In the world of Tolstoy's novel it is no mere prejudice to insist that raising and educating children is a woman's work. Fashionable society's practice of giving children to servants has turned it into a Babylon. Happiness in marriage depends on a woman's growing into her natural duties. But Anna has sacrificed too much to settle for less than passion; she has seen Vronsky disgusted by her when she was pregnant, so she won't and can't have more children.

Dolly compares her circumstances with Anna's: "And however white and beautiful her bare arms are, however beautiful her full figure and her eager face under her black curls, he will find something better still, just as my disgusting, pitiful, and charming husband does" (6:23).

Thus Dolly sees that this fascinatingly beautiful woman, whom she admired for her courage and imagined rapturously happy, is degraded and terribly unhappy. The reader has premonitions of her suicide. She swallows a tumbler of wine mixed with morphine in order to sleep, for the gnawings of her conscience cannot be soothed.

Dolly hurries home to her children, overjoyed to be back in the harness of her maternal duties. This is followed by a coda with a subtle purpose. Anna reads in a variety of subjects: agriculture, architecture, horse breeding, and even sports. She also assists Vronsky in the planning of his hospital. Yet these activities, which give her something to do while making her useful to Vronsky as a helpmate, Tolstoy disparages as stratagems in a power play. She is not credited with having any genuine intellectual motive for these pursuits; they are merely "loving snares in which she tried to hold him fast" (6:25).

The final segment, the provincial elections, is observed through Levin's eyes and is an occasion for satirizing the liberals. What dramatic tension there is derives from the tacit struggle being waged between Vronsky and Anna. Tolstoy's enumerating the daily calendar of events recalls Anna's loneliness and jealousy; from her point of view Vronsky has abandoned her to play politics.

The elections give us a strong whiff of Levin's values. He is a kindred spirit with the old reactionary guard, the sort that live in big unstylish houses and have respectful footmen, house serfs that have stuck to the master, and children that greet their father by kissing his hand. To Levin there is nothing of value in provincial government; in fact, it is bound to become harmful once taken over by so-called liberal noblemen like Vronsky, whose theoretical good has little to do with the reality of the peasants' needs. Real noblemen like Levin, and the old warrior with whom he converses, stick to the land, refusing to sell out to the Ryabinins and their ilk though the noblemen are scarcely making 5 percent profit. They wouldn't dream of transforming the land, as Vronsky does, into a capitalist factory. Class instinct, the true blood of the nobility, binds them as if, Levin exclaims proudly, "we were ancient vestals set to keep some sacred fire going" (6:29).

Throughout the elections, Vronsky is portrayed as being free of harassing tension. He does not think about Anna until recalled by her ruse of sending the message that little Annie is sick. That homecoming, in the final chapter of part 6, ends with Anna's compulsively destructive behavior in bed with him. Having gained a complete reconciliation owing to her power to fascinate and rekindle his passion, she suddenly, without premeditation, dares him to abandon her again in the pursuit of his own interests, igniting in Vronsky's eyes "not merely a cold look but the vindictive look of a man persecuted and made cruel" (6:32).

As noted earlier Anna's self-destructive behavior has attracted the interest of Freudian critics. A key to her personality, according to Armstrong, is that Tolstoy's mother died when he was one-and-a-half years old, and that his diaries are crammed with the evidence of "a constant, but losing battle with his shameful sexual appetites" (1988, 18). Armstrong contends that Tolstoy was haunted by guilt at daring to replace the sacred image of his mother with a real wife and that this anxiety about betraying the mother is the source of Tolstoy's structure in *Anna Karenina*. The double plot represents contrasting depictions of acceptable and unacceptable emotional involvements with women other than the mother. Levin transfers to Kitty the recalled innocence of childhood. "He can only contemplate female figures whose underdeveloped sexuality cannot constitute any kind of threat to the hallowed place occupied by the maternal image" (30). But, Armstrong says, the growing threat of intimate involvement with his child bride causes Levin to despair. She conjectures that Tolstoy introduces Nikolai in an attempt to make sense of Levin's despair, but Nikolai's illness and death is not the real source; it is the thought of the mother being supplanted that is intolerable. Because Kitty is not an "enchanting child forever clutching his arm" (29), the narrative leaps over their honeymoon as something "ugly and shameful" to be erased from memory.

According to Armstrong, monogamy with a child bride is not the only acceptable fantasy resolution to Tolstoy's sexual dilemma. Koznychev and Oblonsky are also acceptable self-projections of the author. Koznychev's story is the fantasy of the "expiatory non-marriage" (46), his rejection of Varenka representing "the idealized negation" (55) of sexual love. Armstrong says that the charming Stiva Oblonsky "teaches a lesson that is antithetical to all his author intended to preach" (185)—the lesson that the family survives best with those capable of double standards and compromise. Stiva, in his way, represents a view of life in which the family remains intact and the mother remains enshrined. This repetition of Tolstoy in Levin, Koznyshev, and Oblonsky tends to mock the values of Levin's story line by creating the effect of parody. This gentle undercutting of the hero, who "becomes an adult" in the farcical episode with Veslovsky—"a husband in the most primitive sense of the word" (47)—and only then is able to turn his mind to other preoccupations, makes ever more ambiguous Tolstoy's depiction of Anna, who represents the intolerable alternative to entrenched patriarchy and service to family.

A chief point of Armstrong's study is to demonstrate that there are no clearcut polarities in Tolstoy's novel. Anna is a projection of Tolstoy's repudiated sexual passion. But through her he also explores his longing for passion, which may be the same as saying he was "courageous enough to explore his own longing for death" (137). Moreover, Tolstoy is not only attracted and repelled by Anna as a sexual figure but as a political force, that is, as a threat to the idea of an entrenched patriarchy. And perhaps just as he undercuts Levin, he also, as Armstrong argues, subverts his own intentions with Anna. "The hierarchy appears to

win only if we read Anna's story as one of retribution against an iso-
lated individual who tried to pit herself against the system; but in reality
the triumph of the 'fallen woman' is proclaimed in the power she exerts
over author, reader, and text" (124).

11

The Bitterness of Ecstasy

Levin in Society □ Levin Meets Anna □ Kitty's Labor □ War
with Vronsky □ Anna's Postmortem □ Suicide

The opening of part 7 encapsulates Anna's story, but with a moralistic
ending. Levin, momentarily infatuated with a sensuous woman, rejects
her for his wife and is rewarded with a son. The idea of the novel as a fire
sermon, a warning against carnal passion, recalls M. S. Gromeka's criticism of the novel, which one might imagine as a series of "thou-shalt-
nots" engraved on Anna's tombstone: thou shalt not destroy a family;
thou shalt not build new happiness on old unhappiness; thou shalt not ignore public opinion; thou shalt not find joy in passion (quoted in
Eikenbaum).

D. H. Lawrence calls Tolstoy's moralizing "a crying falsity and
shame." In killing off Anna, probably "because of profligacy in his youth,
because he had disgusted himself in his own flesh, by excess or by prosti-
tution," Lawrence says, "he degraded himself infinitely, he perjured himself far more than did Peter when he denied Christ" (1936, 479).
Lawrence's blast has a salutary effect, like a strong tonic, when Tolstoy's
views stick in the craw. Tolstoy was opposed to feminism, theories of evolution, experimental science, revolutionary idealism, modern technology and, in general, nineteenth-century culture and thought. However,
the world of the novel, like the mind of the man, is so much more than

his views, as the tragic end of Anna's life is incomparably more than the satiric scenes that begin part 7.

Levin meets Anna and is infatuated with her, blaming this momentary lapse on the dissipating influence of life in Moscow society. The extravagant and useless life of the well-to-do is a contagion, and even the most stolid disciple of Rousseau becomes a little degenerate when he goes "stepping out." Levin's outfitting of his several servants while in Moscow costs "the wages of two laborers for the summer . . . and each a day of hard work from early morning to late evening" (7:2). But after the first blush of sin comes indifference. Levin orders grain sold at a loss to have the money to step out into society in a carriage with two powerful horses, which convey him a quarter of a mile and then stand for four hours.

Tolstoy conducts his hero through a typical day in Moscow society, satirizing everything the town has to offer. University life and culture in general are ridiculous. The professors are like woodpeckers hammering out the same note of their pet theories. Levin attends a concert where the modern music is formless and the talk of connoisseurs is blather. Levin makes a social call. It is expected of him. He sits on a sofa with his hat on his knees, making meaningless conversation for ten minutes, and leaves feeling ashamed and stupid. At a public meeting, a charity, he finds the conversation no more meaningful—pretentious chatter about doing something socially beneficial—in short, a distraction for the rich, like the races. He then gets drunk at an exclusive noblemen's club, where he laughs raucously at off-color jokes, gambles at cards, and even chats amicably with Vronsky. Infected by smoke, drink, food, and gambling, the Tolstoyan hero is ushered from the club to his meeting with Anna.

He gazes at the Mikhailov portrait, astonished by her beauty, and then at Anna, instantly falling under her spell despite the obvious coquettishness and affectation of her manner toward him. "I knew her [Kitty] for a very short time, but she left on me the impression of an exquisite flower, simply a flower. And to think, she will soon be a mother!" (7:10). The breadth of Anna's culture infatuates him: her familiarity with modern art, Doré's illustrations of the Bible, the novels of Zola and Daudet.

The Bitterness of Ecstasy

"'Yes, yes, this is a woman!' Levin thought, forgetting himself and staring persistently at her lovely, mobile face, which at that moment was all at once completely transformed" (7:10).

Anna is playing up to him, and Levin is smitten. Steiner says that "no man will approach Anna with more compassionate insight" (1959, 61) than Levin, but this is a false note. Levin loathes his own sexual needs. He has married a sweet innocent girl, and he will promptly repudiate his infatuation with Anna. This would have been the case even had he been unmarried; for the facts that she may be a remarkable woman and that the fashionable clique that judges her is affected, irreverent, and hypocritical are beside the point. The only point for Levin, although he is not yet aware of it, is that passionate attachments without concern for God are wrong.

The scene with his wife in which he denounces Anna has a prologue in which he shrugs at news from his bailiff that his corn crop has been sold at a loss. Life in fashionable society has made him a little degenerate and, besides, he is infatuated with a magnificent concubine. His blushes before tear-stricken Kitty lead him to honestly confess as much to himself.

Anna confesses to practicing coquetry on Levin because of the war she is engaged in with Vronsky, a war in which she will destroy herself, futilely pitting her power against his will to enjoy independent pursuits. Levin is merely instrumental, a proof to her of her desirability to men. Many critics insist that part of her tragedy comes from Vronsky's inability to understand her. Wasiolek says that "[h]e knows neither what she is doing to herself nor what she is doing to him" (1978, 147). And this view of him is echoed by Nabokov, who suggests that Vronsky's "bland insensitivity" toward Kitty grades "into callousness and even brutality" with Anna (1981, 188). One recalls that during his week away at the elections, he was not once moved by uneasiness on her account. His self-possession is quite secure against guilty misgivings, which from another perspective hardly seems a bad thing. When, meeting hostility after his return from the gentlemen's club, he appeals for tenderness, Anna cannot yield. "But some strange force of evil would not let her give herself up to her feelings, as though the rules of warfare would not permit her to surrender" (7:12). She provokes his hostility, and then appeals for pity because she is terrified by what she is doing. She is playing with death. She acts out the calamity of having strangled Vronsky's love for her. Moved by her despair, he appeals again for tenderness, showing a willingness to concede anything to make her happy. But while this restores the peace, Vronsky resents the power play by which he was forced to make concessions.

Levin once again repudiates his attraction to Anna before experiencing his son's birth. He confesses that he was becoming an insensible brute in Moscow from "leading an aimless, senseless life, living beyond his means . . . drinking to excess . . . forming inappropriately friendly relations" and that his fascination with "a woman who could only be called a fallen woman" (7:13) was the height of degeneracy. The genuineness of his contrition completely reassures Kitty and enables Tolstoy to achieve an effective contrast between the truthful candor of the Levins—Kitty suffering birth pains, pressing Levin's hand to her breast and kissing it— and the operatic and contorted emotions of Anna and Vronsky. One contrast leads to another. Levin, the man of science, the rationalist and nonbeliever, prays to God in his fear for Kitty, and Tolstoy says that his skepticism "floated out of his soul like dust" (7:13).

Levin has no sophisticated defenses. He cannot abstract himself from Kitty's pain. He prays incessantly during her labor, experiencing emotions that were "openings, as it were, in that ordinary life through which there came glimpses of something sublime" (7:14). In this exalted state, from which reason and will are excluded, Levin experiences the convulsions of faith. He too is undergoing labor pains of a kind, and despite "his long and, as it seemed, complete alienation from religion," he will eventually deliver himself "to God just as trustfully and simply as he had in his childhood and first youth" (7:14).

Tolstoy surpasses himself in the venom of his attacks on fashionable society as a preface to Anna's suicide. We hear that Prince Chechensky has two wives and two families and broadens his legitimate son's ideas by taking him to his second family; that Bartnyansky lives with debts amounting to a million and a half; and that Count Krivtsov, also in hopeless debt, keeps two mistresses (7:20).

The Bitterness of Ecstasy

There is a self-serving nastiness in the scene with Landau. Stiva, more concerned with the sinecure he covets than with arranging his sister's divorce, considers tapping Lydia for her influence. Lydia and Karenin preach to him about the happiness faith brings, and the charlatan smiles slyly as he waits to do Lydia's bidding. Babylon and its obscene priestess with her bogus "Christianity" refuse Anna a divorce. Anna is an image of the best that is possible in this debased society where she can find nothing to sustain her. Princess Myakaya says, "Ever since they've all turned against her, all those who're a thousand times worse than she, I've thought she did a very fine thing" (7:20).

The sequence of chapters building to Anna's suicide begins with an account of the state of war between her and Vronsky.

> And being jealous of him, Anna was indignant against him and found grounds for indignation in everything. For everything that was difficult in her position she blamed him. . . . If he had loved her he would have seen all the bitterness of her position, and would have rescued her from it. For her being in Moscow and not in the country, he was to blame too. He could not live buried in the country as she would have liked to do. He had to have society, and he had put her in this awful position, the bitterness of which he would not see. And again, it was his fault that she was forever separated from her son. (7:23)

It is a vicious circle: blaming the man whose love she desperately needs for the misery she feels, which can only be consoled by his love; resenting him bitterly for the cooling of his passion, conscious that the compulsion to blame him is the cause of his coolness; imagining death to be the only way out of her predicament; terrified by her imaginings and clutching at him the more desperately; rekindling his passion and immediately attacking him again. Their relationship has become fraught with occasions for conflict because Vronsky is free and she is an outcast, and because he is constitutionally strong-willed whereas she has been psychically crippled, the pariah dependent on his love. In their recent quarrel we hear only Anna's side. Vronsky has mocked the idea of girls being tutored in physics and called Anna's tutoring of the subject unnatural. This attack mortifies her because in her mind it can only be a symptom of his cooling

love, a cruel sneer at her efforts to give some meaning to the socially intolerable position he has put her in. Yet she has no idea of the venom in
her attacks on him for his civic zeal. He has the power to leave her; what
is her strength compared to *his*? Indeed, she considers only that he does
strike, which must mean that his love for her has cooled and that he loves
someone else.

Anna is frightened by her behavior. She is capable of seeing herself
clearly—he loves nobody but me; I'm exceedingly irritable; I've got to get
hold of myself. But her perception grows increasingly distorted—I'm revolting; he loves the young Princess Sorokina; I'll make him pay. She
knows this perception is distorted but cannot help yielding to it and provoking Vronsky to exasperation. There is only a short step from cutting
the last tie to fantasizing about suicide. "Yes, to die! . . . And the shame
and disgrace of Aleksey Aleksandrovich and of Seryozha, and my terrible
shame, it will all be saved by death. To die! And he will feel remorse; will
be sorry; will love me; he will suffer on my account" (7:24). Then, terrified by her obsessive fantasies, she becomes hysterical. "What am I? An
immoral woman! A stone around your neck. I don't want to make you
wretched; I don't want to! I'll set you free. You don't love me; you love
someone else!" (7:24). Vronsky's tender reassurances are temporarily
convincing. Anna covers his face and hands with kisses in despairing
passion.

The critics who feel superior to Vronsky, blaming him for callousness and for being merely ordinary, are behaving like Levin, forgetting
themselves in their infatuation with Anna. She is determined on catastrophe, and a better man than Vronsky (however this "better" is to be
interpreted by the critics who judge him) would have been just as ineffec-
tual and probably more cruel. Anna is compulsively willing her own destruction as the means "of punishing him and of gaining the victory in
that strife which the evil spirit in possession of her heart was waging with
him" (7:26).

Tolstoy marks the point after which she is locked in her embittered,
paranoid monologue by assaulting her with a twofold onslaught of terror.
Her candle blows out, chilling her soul with an evil premonition, and then
she is wakened from a drugged sleep by the old nightmare of the hideous

peasant with the dirty beard. This time the dream has an eerie nearness to prophecy. In his "doing something bent down over some iron" (7:26), we can almost make out the rails and her mutilated body. What makes it horrible to Anna is the premonition that she is dead in her dream, "that this peasant was taking no notice of her, but was doing something horrible with the iron—over her." She has had this dream many times, "even before her liaison with Vronsky" (7:26). How odd that Tolstoy has not told us this earlier! For Anna to experience the dream before her affair implies that her longing for passion preceded her affair with Vronsky and that the violent death augured by the dream is inevitable.

She goes down to his study to be reconciled with him, but the imprint of death is on her soul. As she passes through the drawing room, a carriage pulls up to the door and Vronsky is handed a packet from the young Princess Sorokina. Her distorted perception—Vronsky loves someone young and fresh; I'll make him pay—overwhelms her. But she would have been overwhelmed in any case. It is impossible for Anna not to see in the flux of circumstance cause for humiliation and despairing jealousy.

Tottering from the succession of blows, she stands before her mirror gazing at her swollen face with glittering eyes. "'Why, it's me!' she suddenly understood, and looking around, she seemed all at once to feel his kisses on her, and twitched her shoulders, shuddering. Then she lifted her hand to her lips and kissed it. 'What is it? Why, I'm going out of my mind!'" (7:27). Thus the link between Vronsky's passion and her madness having been magically soldered, Anna is locked in the dislocation from reality that ends in her suicide.

During Anna's carriage ride to Dolly's, her thoughts shift from the humiliation of her dependency to the intention of making him pay. "'I won't give in to him; I won't let him train me as he pleases. . . . How conceited and self-satisfied he will be when he gets my note! . . . Longing for humiliation again!' she said to herself. . . . 'These horses, this carriage—how loathsome I am to myself in this carriage—all his; but I won't see them again'" (7:28).

Fear keeps her going. She has the consciousness of a person condemned to death, looking out at the world with reproach, imprecations, and embittered, despairing cynicism. She is the pariah in her scene with Dolly and Kitty, and it is chillingly plain, says Bayley, how casually and completely even those given to sympathize with her have come to accept her isolation. "It is her sense of being outcast from the kind of society in which she is most naturally at home, and where at the beginning of the book she was at home, that gives Anna her final despair" (1966, 227).

Maddened by "vague fury and craving for revenge" (7:29), Anna determines to make a scene at Vronsky's mother's, to catch her lover in the act with the young Princess Sorokina, and then to do away with herself. Her postmortem on her relationship with Vronsky has the insightfulness of something seen in absolute despair and is true within the limits of a life devoid of all supports but love. Her perceptions have a logic to them, a logic that is dictated not only by circumstances, but also by a conscience that is driving her to the ultimate punishment.

"Yes, there was the triumph of success in him. Of course there was love too, but the chief element was the pride of success. He boasted of me. . . . He is weary of me and is trying not to be dishonorable in his behavior toward me. . . . [H]e wants divorce and marriage so as to burn his ships. He loves me, but how? The zest is gone, as the English say. . . . My love keeps growing more passionate and selfish, while his is dying, and that's why we're drifting apart. . . . If I could be anything but a mistress, passionately caring for nothing but his caresses; but I can't and I don't care to be anything else. And by that desire I rouse aversion in him, and he rouses fury in me, and it cannot be different. Don't I know that he wouldn't deceive me, that he has no schemes about Princess Sorokina, that he's not in love with Kitty, that he won't desert me! I know all that, but it makes it no easier for me. If without loving me, from duty he'll be good and kind to me, without what I want, that's a thousand times worse than unkindness! That's—hell! And that's just how it is. . . . And is there any new feeling I can awaken between Vronsky and me? Is there possible, if not happiness, some sort of ease from misery? No, no!" she answered now without the slightest hesitation. "Impossible! We are drawn apart by life, and I make his unhappiness and he mine, and there's no changing him or me. Every attempt has been made, but the screw has lost its thread." (7.30)

The Bitterness of Ecstasy

There is no way out for Anna. People are hideous; life itself is hideous; everything in the passing scene is repulsive. Everything is deceit, lies, and vanity.

At the station platform where Vronsky has left the Moscow train to see his mother, Anna hears from a porter that Princess Sorokina has just left by carriage for Madame Vronsky's. The Vronsky's coachman delivers a note repeating Vronsky's previous message that he's tied up till ten. There is no reprieve. Anna throws herself under a freight train.

12

Tolstoy's "Animal Metaphysicum"

Patriotic Failures □ Vronsky's Prostration □ Negative
Obituaries □ Levin's Epiphany □ The Closure of the Novel

The epilogue opens with a disapproving picture of the volunteers' move-ment to help the Balkan Slavs. By ridiculing these men as failures, Tolstoy effectively etches an epigraph to Vronsky's life, for he is one of them. Koznyshev, one of the promoters of the volunteers' movement, needs the cause célèbre in order to forget the failure of his book. Another enthusi-ast, Stiva Oblonsky, makes his curtain call at the platform of the train where the volunteers are being given a send-off. He appears stale and tire-some, too busy enjoying life to shed tears for his sister who has been dead for two months. The charming manner is distasteful after the emotional impact of Anna's suicide.

Tolstoy does not dramatize Vronsky's life during the two months following Anna's suicide. Part 7 ends with Anna's death; part 8 resolves Levin's doubts. Once again Tolstoy uses a train as a vehicle for violent passions. A train brought Anna to Moscow and back to Petersburg with Vronsky following; a train carried Levin to Western Europe in profound despair; the hotel in which Nikolai died had a "modern up-to-date self-complacent railway uneasiness" (5:17); Anna throws her life away under a train; and in part 8 Vronsky is traveling to the war by train, determined to destroy himself.

Tolstoy's "Animal Metaphysicum"

Tolstoy wrote Turgenev in 1857 that "the railroad is to travel as the whore is to love" (Jahn 1981, 1), and commentators have suggested that behind the train symbolism in the novel was Tolstoy's belief that "the railroad served only to pander to and further inflame the already monstrous appetite of the idle and privileged for foreign luxuries" (1), a development certain to destroy the position of the landowning nobility. Thus the underlying emotional referent of this negative symbolism— suggesting evil and destructive power—is Tolstoy's identification of trains with "the brute intrusion of the modern into a traditional way of life" (2). Trains in Anna Karenina are identified with death and illicit sex.

Vronsky and Koznyshev pace back and forth in the shadow of sacks piled on the station platform. Anna is evoked by this scene. She'd have been carried away in one of those sacks. The peasant in her nightmare was doing something with a sack (4:3), and the implication is that *that something* had to do with her mutilated body. Vronsky feels her presence on the platform and bursts into sobs. His prostration does him credit. He prowls the platform "like a wild beast in a cage" (8:5), his face aged from suffering. An implacable anger poisons his memories of Anna. It's like the raging toothache from which he is free only when overcome by a rare flood of remorse. She had said when they last quarreled that he would be sorry and here he is, good for nothing but for throwing away his life.

Two negative obituaries follow, one bitterly spoken by Vronsky's mother. "'Yes, hers was the fitting end for such a woman. Even the death she chose was coarse and vulgar. . . . No, say what you will, she was a bad woman. . . . She brought herself to ruin and two good men—her husband and my unhappy son'" (8:4). The second obituary is implicit in the transitional chapter that describes Kitty nursing her son. Kitty knows by the flow of her milk that her baby is crying. The mother is bonded to the child, Tolstoy says, by "a whole series of spiritual relations" (8:6). Anna, having broken those bonds, pays the supreme penalty.

The final movement of the novel, in which Levin resolves his doubts, also begins with a contrast to Anna. Whereas she had broken the maternal bond and the bond of duty to her husband, Levin is the lifeline for an extended family. But, although his life is valuable to others—to family, to kin, and to the peasants working his farm—it has no meaning at all to him. He has been profusely blessed by good fortune, yet is terrified about the inevitability of death. Levin never asks whether his dread of death is pathological. That other nonbelievers fail to draw the conclusions that horrify him strikes him as pathological. "In infinite time, in infinite matter, in infinite space, is formed a bubble-organism, and that bubble lasts a while and bursts, and that bubble is I" (8:9). This conclusion is forced on him by the science of his age. But he also believes that this reasonable idea can't be right. "It was an agonizing fallacy. . . . But it was not merely a fallacy, it was the cruel jest of some wicked power, some evil, hateful power, to whom one could not submit" (8:9).

Here Tolstoy somewhat resembles Dostoyevsky, who stages morality plays in which atheist heroes, men of reason, struggle with good and evil angels. The good angel (conscience, intuition) inspires love of humanity and belief in the supernatural. The evil angel (intellect, energy) commands the fascination and delight of the reader. In these morality plays, the good angel proves that life is insupportable without belief in God. Dostoyevsky's characters undergo mental breakdowns on account of the tortured split caused by this warfare. "And Levin, a happy father and husband, in perfect health, was several times so near suicide that he hid a rope so that he might not be tempted to hang himself, and was afraid to go out with his gun for fear of shooting himself" (8:9).

But Levin experiences an epiphany. Fyodor, one of his peasants, says that Mitiukh lives only for filling his belly, but Fokanych lives for his soul, "in truth, in God's way" (8:11), and Levin realizes that he has been attempting to live like Fokanych. His revulsion against the Babylon of town life, his longing for chastity, his attempts, through Kitty, to get back to his childhood faith, his theory of agriculture—in all these ways, without knowing it, he has been living for God.

Levin feels astounded by this miraculous discovery. It is comprehensible and rational for men to live for their bellies. As rational beings, men can do nothing else. Yet the vast majority of men of all times and places know infallibly what they must live for and what is good. Fyodor's words, and the realization that the force directing life works in opposition to reason, carries Levin on a crest of spiritual excitement to a sense of freedom from despair.

"I have found the Master" (8:12). This "Master" provides the answer, and the only answer, to death. The pride of intellect had nearly been his ruin, leaving him with the conclusion that life was "the evil mockery of some devil" (8:12). But Levin sees that while one can't reason oneself to belief in God, yet the knowledge of what is right and what is wrong, which every man is given to know infallibly, is incontestable proof of God's existence.

Levin concludes that all his life he had been living rightly, although thinking wrongly. "Yes, what I know, I know not by reason, but it has been given to me, revealed to me, and I know it with my heart, by faith in the chief thing taught by the church" (8:13). He watches a herd of cattle crossing over to drink at the river and is disturbed by the unconscious thought: was he to be led thus? However, the sweep of his spiritual excitement carries him past his former doubts to the chief thing—"faith in God, in goodness, as the one goal of man's destiny" (8:13). He believes that he can accept all the church doctrines, that all were established for one purpose—to strengthen men in the conviction that they should be living, not for their bellies, but for the life of the soul.

This new, important event in Levin's life is the note upon which the novel closes. Ostensibly, nothing has changed. He's as quick to lose his temper and is as opinionated as ever. The newness about him is his feeling of spiritual peace. Life is no longer meaningless; it has the "unquestionable meaning of the goodness" (8:19) that his hope of salvation has given him power to put into it.

Henry Gifford says of this closure, "What [Tolstoy] had not known profoundly himself but had merely aspired to know he could not make convincing in his fictional characters" (1982, 52). He says Levin's conversion is unconvincing because Tolstoy himself, despite his desperate efforts, could not believe in the Church's doctrines. "He longed to stifle the voice of his rationality, even though the faith he envied was inseparable from superstitions" (46). Ultimately he failed, "revolted by the Church's exclusive claim to truth, by its intolerance, by its readiness to support war in the national interest. Finally he was driven to make his own study of the scriptures, resulting in two declarations of independence: *A Criticism of Dogmatic Theology* [1880] and *A Translation and Harmony of the Four Gospels* [1883]" (46).

In the exposition of his faith in 1884, Tolstoy asserted his disbelief in personal resurrection and immortality. To make the spiritual realm of Christ a kingdom on *earth* was his mission. Tolstoy interpreted the Church's teaching about reward and punishment to mean that a life dedicated to doing good for its own sake is everlasting, that the good man is rewarded with fearlessness in the face of death. In comparison with this genuine spiritual struggle—Tolstoy's crisis, described in *Confession* (1879–82) and culminating in *What I Believe* (1884)—Gifford finds Levin's spiritual peace illegitimate, poorly portrayed, because Tolstoy couldn't believe in the doctrines of the Church.

Tolstoy's emphatic rejection of traditional Christian salvation inevitably influences the way commentators see Levin. Gary Jahn uses Tolstoy's later faith in the earthly kingdom of God to explain the novel's close as a stage in an unfolding process of enlightenment. Levin has discovered the spiritual life, what he calls on the last page of the novel the soul's "holy of holies," and to the extent that he is able to "remove from his life every vestige of dissonance with the commands of the spirit" (1985, 479), his terror of death is diminished. Jahn traces an evolution of increasing freedom from the "animal life" in the heroes of Tolstoy's three major novels, treating Levin as the halfway point on the way to Nekhlyudov of *Resurrection* (1899).

It is difficult to look at Levin without seeing Tolstoy in the midst of his spiritual crisis. Levin's search for religious values is undoubtedly autobiographical. But it is one thing to say that Levin is Tolstoy and another thing to explain Levin in terms of beliefs that Tolstoy held years later. In the mid-1870s Tolstoy was trying to come to terms with the traditional Christian belief in personal immortality. The main actions of Levin's life are unconscious bids for personal immortality, which he isn't able to admit to himself because, until the novel's end, he isn't able to admit that he believes in God. There is a pressure, a momentum, to his need to believe in and feel worthy of salvation, which Tolstoy resolves by having Levin choose faith over science. In the context of the novel we are left with a question: Do we believe in his having come through, or are we left with a sense of compression, of unfinished action, with the feeling that the end does not resolve Levin's problem?

13

Conclusion

When Thomas Hardy writes, "The crash of broken commandments is as necessary an accompaniment to the catastrophe of a tragedy as the noise of drum and cymbal to a triumphant march" (1966, 129), he means that an artist whose brain is afire with the story of passion will of necessity magnify the force and terror of traditional moral law. Thus, in *Anna Karenina*, Tolstoy's representation of Levin's life as the right life, a life of moral dignity, is set in opposition to Anna's catastrophic passion. Levin embodies the morality that Anna violates; the double plot is a narrative device, a means of illuminating Anna's tragedy and Levin's salvation. Yet Anna's loveless marriage to a frigid husband, which Tolstoy paints with acid strokes, compels our sympathy; we admire her and at the same time see that Tolstoy has no patience for the cultured society that judges her. Society has a negative effect on human nature; it is based on expedience and represents the power of the majority over the individual. Only in part does Anna's sense of guilt derive from her position as a "fallen woman."

Readers familiar with Tolstoy's artistic development, who see the genesis of the novel in the context of his life and times, read in the conflict between asceticism and passion a personal struggle that was coming to resolution. Thomas Mann calls *Anna Karenina* "a signpost on the woeful way of the cross the poet was taking" ("Anna Karenina," 181). Knowing that after writing the novel Tolstoy had a religious conversion that resulted in a revulsion against literature and that Levin is, by and large, the author's self-portrait, Mann defends Anna against Tolstoy's darkening religiosity by attacking the odious tendencies he sees in Levin's views.

Tolstoy, who was nearing fifty when he wrote *Anna Karenina*, was a man with an extremely forceful nature. His position in regard to the feminine role was thoroughly traditional; it can be found in Proverbs 31:10 and 28. "Who can find a virtuous woman? for her price is far above rubies. . . . Her children arise up, and call her blessed; her husband also, and he praiseth her." Tolstoy's ideal of woman as fruitful mother and obedient wife distorts his treatment of Anna. Indeed, the moral bias of the novel is largely the product of forces that shaped the man—his affinity to certain doctrines of philosophy, the crisis of faith he was undergoing, and his political and emotional stance on the issues of his time.

Rousseau was the shaper of Tolstoy's youth, Schopenhauer of his middle years, the deeply depressed years (1869–79) just before, during, and after the writing of *Anna Karenina*. Tolstoy once remarked: "I have read the whole of Rousseau—all his twenty volumes, including his *Dictionary of Music*. . . . At the age of fifteen I wore a medallion portrait of him next to my body instead of the Orthodox cross. Many of his pages are so akin to me that it seems to me that I must have written them myself" (Maude 1930, 1:49).

The tone of Rousseau's work is that of an outsider with a message for humanity. The moral scheme of *Anna Karenina* illustrates the main points of this message. Society is wicked, man is by nature good. European culture sacrifices the innate moral harmony of man to artificially uniform behavior. Man is alienated from his original nature and prevented from being his real self. The more splendid the social culture, the weaker genuine human relationships. Idleness and vanity will divert a woman from her natural modesty to shameless indulgence in passion. Since civilization is the corrupting force and vice is introduced from outside, it follows that rural environments are superior to urban ones. Tolstoy, like Rousseau, hated European civilization, and, like Rousseau, believed the laws of nature were primary. Rousseau's panegyric on family life in *La Nouvelle Héloïse* appealed to Tolstoy's deepest convictions. In *Anna Karenina* he extends this ideal of family life to include the traditional ties bonding landowners to their peasants.

This contrast between life in fashionable society with its sophisticated splendor and life on the land with its natural simplicity is fundamentally, on the moral plane of *Anna Karenina*, a contrast between evil and good. The double plot plays off this contrast. The salon life of Petersburg makes Anna's adultery convenient. The land is a source of spiritual regeneration to those capable of receiving its sustenance, and it imposes on Levin an obligation to protect it. Anna, whose adultery is encouraged by high society, progressively disengages herself from all concerns but sexual love. She is alone, defenseless, and death-driven, and her agony touches us; but Levin, increasingly bound up with people who are dependent on him, and always troubled about how to improve his usefulness, follows the way of nature—a country road. The way of the world is the way of damnation.

But while Rousseau's ideas are persuasive, the influence of Schopenhauer is also present in Tolstoy's thought. Man is not merely the victim of harmful influences; suffering and evil are inherent in the nature of things. The intellect is a tool of the will, its mouthpiece, serving to rationalize the instincts; and this will, which drives every human life, is a compulsive and insatiable force. Life, as Schopenhauer describes it, is pure hell, for the will is always disappointed. Fulfilled desire creates satiety, a new vacancy, a new rage. Sexual appetite is the most destructive symptom of a diseased will, a demon and the source of enormous suffering. Schopenhauer rejected such ideas as human progress and the perfectibility of man. The science of the age could change nothing, since evil derives from man himself. Since the will is life, there can be no release from passion except in death or in going beyond desire through asceticism and self-denial.

From the perspective of this celebrated doctrine, the moral scheme of *Anna Karenina* appears to be a contrast between two lives: one that is driven by passion to imagine that happiness is the attainment of desire, the other driven by despair to find peace in religious conversion. Anna's suffering derives from the nature of passion. The loss of respectability, social ostracism, the longing for her son—these are secondary to the insatiability of the will, which is the central tragedy of human life. The Levin plot demonstrates that earthly life can be complete and satisfying; it exemplifies Tolstoy's moral law: thou shalt live in the country, work hard, be dutiful to family, renounce passion, and believe in God. His point seems to be that people are made miserable by the combined efforts of destiny and society when they disobey any part of this law.

It certainly appears that Tolstoy's own great gift for life, the passion and stamina that poured itself into *War and Peace* (1863–69), struck him increasingly as a hindrance. After the gloomy summer with Schopenhauer (whom he read in 1869), he became depressed. The inevitability of death tormented him. What could satisfy his spirits and his hopes if all endeavors were futile? The writing of *Anna Karenina*, which he began in 1873, struck him as banal. The labor was so distasteful that it made him ill, and he pushed it aside for months at a time during the four years of its genesis. Tolstoy was headed for a total breakdown. Under the pressure of this oncoming crisis, which was subsequently released in religious writing, he took solace in the story of Levin, whose search for meaning is his own.

Levin confesses that it is impossible for a rationalist and natural scientist like himself to believe in God, and yet his chief traits and actions testify to an unconscious longing for God—his hatred of the Babylon of city life, his rebirth of the soul when returning to the land, his efforts at chastity, his attraction to the sweet and innocent Kitty, and his guilt at being a landlord and exploiter. He ends by realizing that he had been seeking salvation all along. He had been living, without knowing it, as if life were exceedingly difficult without God. Anna, by contrast, dies because she's unable to sublimate her sexual passion. Sex is a destructive rather than a life-giving force, and the double plot of the novel offers two alternatives for Levin and Anna, that is, for strong personalities who are forthright and passionate—faith or suicide.

But *Anna Karenina*, while it was the harbinger of momentous changes in Tolstoy's life, was also his political challenge to the intelligentsia of his time. Tolstoy was a country squire, one of the old hereditary gentry, who regarded his peasants as his moral responsibility. Paternalism was a sacred trust, implying both the landowner's right to assert authority and his obligation to take care of his peasants. By glorifying the paternal ideal that bonded landowner and peasant, by mocking Westernizers and warning against their social theories and progressive ideas, Tolstoy, in his pedagogical writings and his great works of literature as well, makes a powerful defense of his class interest. The radical intelligentsia regarded him as a reactionary for his opposition to social reform. He was, as well, a troglodyte in his attitude toward women. Their work was to raise children and nothing else, and if they had no children, he instructed them to become nannies. Anna is distorted by this attitude, and Vronsky, Oblonsky, and Koznyshev are contrasted with Levin, who embodies a traditional, patriarchal ideology.

The form of the novel is designed to keep our feelings and thoughts continuously stirred and unsettled, especially in regard to the powerful figure who gives the novel its name. Anna is a fascinating woman and superior to all the others in her elite social set, but while we feel drawn to her and can't help identifying with her, the novel's form exerts a steady pressure of resistance to our sympathy, a pressure, that is, of disapproval and condemnation. This is achieved by means of the alternating double plot in which right love is counterpointed against wrong love: while the one is blossoming, the other is disintegrating. Moral pressure is exerted at certain touch points or connecting links between the two stories, as well as through the patterning of the segments themselves in which essentially the same psychological situation is repeated with a different moral emphasis. For instance, in part 5, Levin's fear of death strengthens his union with Kitty, leading, in part 7, to the birth of a son; Anna, in part 6, having abandoned her son, exasperates Vronsky to heighten his ardor. Fear of death tightens their union also, and leads, in part 7, to her suicide. Levin's jealous fits in part 6 express his vexation with Kitty for not being able to allay his fear of death; similarly, Anna rages at Vronsky for not allaying her despair. In the "right" union jealousy is farcical; in the "wrong" union it is devastating. The opening of part 7 retells Anna's story through Levin who, corrupted by society, becomes infatuated with her; Levin is rewarded for not succumbing to his passion for a sensuous woman, whereas Anna, who has succumbed to passion, kills herself.

Although Tolstoy tries to make passion hideous and Christian love supreme, Anna, whenever she appears, is wonderful, even noble, and most of the other characters are feeble things beside her. Since Tolstoy cannot quite believe in his hero's religious conversion and cannot deprecate passion, his conflict creates a subtle, vibrating, delicate balance, which is the secret of the novel's mysterious richness. The overall effect is of a divided mind, as if, George Steiner says, "two deities have been invoked, an ancient patriarchal god of vengeance, and a god who sets nothing above the tragic candor of a bruised spirit" (1959, 282).

But aside from the various ways in which the poetic form of the novel neutralizes Tolstoy's didactic purpose, a certain remarkable aspect of his narration seems to obliterate moral distinctions and make them irrelevant. His omniscient eye is clear-sightedly detached, relating everything with the same evenness of tone. Tolstoy the Rousseauian describes rustic scenes vividly, especially in the sacramental moments—Levin mowing with the peasants, watching the stars through the night, hunting snipe at dawn, etc. But equally vivid, and remarkably free of venom and caricature, are his descriptions of fashionable society, for example, in the striking picture of Anna's indiscreet behavior with Vronsky as she exits late at night from Betsy's salon. "A footman stood opening the carriage door. The hall porter stood holding open the great door of the house. Anna Arkadyevna, with her quick little hand, was unfastening the lace of her sleeve, caught in the hook of her fur cloak, and, with bent head, listening with rapture to the words Vronsky murmured as he escorted her down" (2:7). For the better part he describes this opulent world with the same equanimity and vividness as he does nature—with the same comprehensive gaze as that with which Homer shows us Menelaus and Helen enthroned in the *Odyssey*.

Yet what effect has this equanimity on the reader when, without feeling but with icy brilliance, he describes Anna's last day, looking through her as if she were transparent, looking into every cranny of her thoughts? Some think it cruel, the anger of a patriarch at a sinful woman or the bitterness of the spirit against the flesh, yet it is this characteristic epic cast of mind, a comprehensiveness of vision, that sets Tolstoy apart from all other novelists.

But not only do the realism of his epic narration and the ambiguity he creates through his poetic form resist his moral biases, he also has made Anna too powerfully appealing for him to control her. The artist in him couldn't bring himself merely to sacrifice her to his animus; instead, he created mystery by making her psychology so remarkably interesting that readers continue to muse on the meaning of her tragic fate.

Dostoyevsky, for example, was struck by Anna's egotism and selfishness, with its pitiable flicker of rationality. But he says nothing of Anna's beauty or any other redeeming features. To him she is a profound illustration of society's need for God (Gifford 1971, 51–52).

Indeed, everybody with an ax to grind discovers in Anna's story a case in point. D. H. Lawrence chastises Tolstoy for knuckling under to a dead ideology and branding Anna with a sense of sin that is not essential to her nature; he charges Tolstoy with immorality for not having the courage to celebrate her passion.

George Steiner says "Tolstoy's genius was inexhaustibly literal" (1959, 274) and that if he had any shortcomings, it was the price he paid for realism—namely, his inability to convey the mystery of the irrational. But it is precisely this mystery that Tolstoy grasped in the creation of Anna, and his achievement makes this novel special.

Nabokov says that Tolstoy's characters live like the characters in no other author because his "prose keeps pace with our pulses" (1981, 142), in other words, that the time values in the novel correspond in some miraculous way with our sense of time. What is true is the incomparable artistry of the novel—the poetry of its architecture, the epic grandeur of its realism, and its inimitable characterization.

Perspectives on the Novel

D. H. *Lawrence*

Lawrence's reflections on *Anna Karenina* are scattered throughout his writings. In his view, Tolstoy betrays Anna by not giving her enough strength to fight society on equal terms. He creates her "with a definite weakness . . . a certain inevitable and inconquerable adhesion to the community" (1936, 439), denying thereby his own instinct for life, which should transcend any theory of right and wrong. Anna cannot detach herself from society because she cannot bear the isolation and exposure and is pulled down; and the real tragedy of the novel, he says, is that she is "unfaithful to the greater unwritten morality, which would have bidden Anna Karenina be patient and wait until she, by virtue of greater right, could take what she needed from society; would have bidden Vronsky detach himself from the system, become an individual, creating a new colony of morality with Anna" (1936, 420). For, Lawrence says, "one must bide by the best that one has known, and not succumb to the lesser good" (1936, 420). And "let it be a great passion and then death, rather than a false or faked purpose" (1960, 220).

Lawrence declared war on an entire culture, believing that morality must of necessity be revolutionary. He read literature as a diagnosis of Western man's mutilated psyche and regarded his task as a literary critic "to save the tale from the artist who created it" (1923, 3). He holds the doctrine of *Anna Karenina* to be blasphemous, because Tolstoy succumbs to a dead ideology. Lawrence's quarrel with Tolstoy is, in the deeper sense, not with the artist but with Christian culture that causes him to go wrong and, by betraying Anna, to betray the truer implications of his work.

He is angry with Tolstoy for doing to Anna, whom he regards as a greater creation than any of Shakespeare's women (Nehls 1959, 3, 113), what writers throughout the nineteenth century consistently did to their flesh and blood heroines—destroy them. Either they are split in two, as in Cooper's *Deerslayer*, where the passionate and dark heroine is unworthy and her fairhaired, simple sister is good; or they are denied their sexuality, as in Charlotte Brontë's *Jane Eyre*, where the heroine is permitted to feel sexual desire only after her Rochester is maimed. Often these characters are branded and made to suffer a sense of sin foisted upon them by the author, as Hawthorne's and Hardy's women, Hester Prynne and Tess. All these writers, by failing to transcend their culture, Lawrence believes, are guilty of immorality. "When the novelist puts his thumb in the scale to pull down the balance to his own predilections, that is immorality" (1936, 528). This is what Tolstoy is guilty of when he attributes to Anna and Vronsky a fatal fear of society and then exploits their tragedy for a didactic purpose.

> Vronsky sinned, did he? But also the sinning was a consummation devoutly to be wished. The novel makes that obvious: in spite of old Leo Tolstoi. . . . There you have the greatness of [the genre of] the novel itself. It won't *let* you tell didactic lies, and put them over. Nobody in the world is anything but delighted when Vronsky gets Anna Karenina. Then what about the sin?—Why, when you look at it, all the tragedy comes from Vronsky's and Anna's fear of *society*. The monster was social, not phallic at all. They couldn't live in the pride of their sincere passion, and spit in Mother Grundy's eye. And that, that cowardice, was the real "sin." The novel makes it obvious, and knocks all old Leo's teeth out. . . . And old Leo tries to make out, it was all because of the phallic sin. Old liar! Because where would any of Leo's books be, without the phallic splendour? And then to blame the column of

blood, which really gave him all his life's riches! . . . It is such a bore that nearly all great novelists have a didactic purpose, otherwise a philosophy, directly opposite to their passional inspiration. In their passional inspiration, they are all phallic worshippers. . . . Yet all of them, when it comes to their philosophy, or what they think-they-are, they are all crucified Jesuses. What a bore! And what a burden for the novel to carry! (1963, 104–6).

Lawrence believes that Tolstoy really loved Anna for her warm-blooded, passionate individuality, and he contends that the novel's morality is not found in Levin but in Anna—in Tolstoy's passionate faith that "our destiny lies in the strength of our desire" (1962, 1:344).[18]

To rescue the tale of the rebellious woman from Tolstoy (and from the other writers who had betrayed her) was central to Lawrence's life, his fiction, and his literary criticism. He eloped with a married woman in the spring of 1912, the mother of three children, and they made a life together in exile, doing what Tolstoy could not permit Anna and Vronsky to do. True, Lawrence had, as Leavis says, an "extraordinary, inexhaustible, and endlessly inquiring intelligence"; true, he never felt "disoriented, vaguely lost, hanging in the wind" (1967, 23) like Vronsky in Italy. But Lawrence's quarrel with Tolstoy is, as mentioned, not so much with the artist of *Anna Karenina* as with the moralist who denied his heroine the courage of her deepest desires. Lawrence's complaint is that Tolstoy ought to have had the courage to write a Lawrentian novel. Ursula of *The Rainbow* (1915) and *Women in Love* (1920), Lou Witt of *St. Mawr* (1924), and Kate Leslie of *The Plumed Serpent* (1926) are heroines who struggle to achieve emotional independence. They aren't afraid of exposure and isolation like Anna; they find out what they really desire and whether or not they have the inner strength to be receptive to it. Indeed, there is a germ of truth to the exaggeration that Lawrence's major fiction is one long corrective to *Anna Karenina*. Connie Chatterley in his last novel, *Lady Chatterley's Lover* (1929), throws over a baronet and an existence that was a "false and faked purpose" to cast her lot with Oliver Mellors. It is the Anna–Karenin–Vronsky story all over again, but this time it is a sheer celebration of the "phallic splendour" of life.

Thomas Mann

Mann acknowledges his indebtedness to Dmitri Merejkowski, *Tolstoi as Man and Artist* (1902), who calls Tolstoy "the great seer of the body" (1902, 213) and extols his sensuous power and pagan genius, while ridiculing his efforts to spiritualize his life and his failure to render those efforts artistically. "[B]ecause of Tolstoi's *too great sense of the body* and too little sense of the spirit" (225), says Merejkowski, his heroes' quests for religious truths are stilted and unconvincing. He regards Tolstoy's conversion as intellectual suicide and laments that "[p]recisely where he sees his shame and shortcoming"—that is, his attachment to the body and to the physical world—"lies his glory and justification" (238).

Mann wrote on Tolstoy in 1922 ("Goethe and Tolstoi"), in 1928 ("Tolstoi [On the Hundredth Anniversary of His Birth]"), and in 1939 ("*Anna Karenina*"). Yasnaya Polyana became a shrine to pilgrims, Mann says, not because Tolstoy was a holy man and founder of a sect but because they wanted "contact with great vital energy, with human nature richly endowed, with the lofty nobility of a beloved child of God" ("Goethe and Tolstoi", 106–7). Mann admires Tolstoy the colossus, the pagan, whose gift of plastic creation, of epic and primeval power, was matchless. His "*penchant* for utopias, his hatred of civilization, his passion for rusticity, for a bucolic placidity of the soul" (98), is Rousseau writ large. He is a son of the earth like the giant Antaeus: when "the strength of his mother the earth streams through him" (117), he creates waves of piercing sensuous enjoyment of nature, which break upon the reader—"streams of refreshment, power, primeval health and a lust of creation" (1928, 159). To Mann, "the sheer *elan* of his creative on-slaught" (160) is of the essence of nature—a radiation of life.

But what perverseness, Mann inquires, what "inimical spirit of contradictiousness" (1922, 134) lies behind Tolstoy's tearing at the bonds of his genius? He attempts to divorce himself from nature, from everything that was natural, "from all the passions of the senses and the instincts, from love, the hunt, at bottom from all of physical life, and especially from art, which meant to him quite essentially the life of the body and the senses" (110–11).

As an attempt to give a moral significance to his life and his art, Tolstoy's later Christianity, says Mann, is pathetic and unconvincing. "Tolstoy's critical and moral faculty, in short his bias toward spirit, was but secondary, an act of will, and a feeble will at that" (115). Mann thinks that Tolstoy never quite succeeded in believing his "Christian, Buddhistic, Chinese gospel of wisdom" (106). He is a "great moralizing infant" in whose "'holiness' a penetrating eye can see so much self-deception, childishness, and 'let's pretend'" (141).

What led to these "naive and clumsy efforts at spiritual regeneration" (115)? It is the fear of death, which has always been in him. "Tolstoy's strongest, most tormenting, deepest, and most productive interest has to do with death. It is the thought of death that dominates his thoughts and writing, to such an extent that one may say no other great master of literature has felt and depicted death as he has—felt it with such frightful penetration, depicted it so insatiably often. . . . Death is a very sensual, very physical business" (155).[19] With *Anna Karenina* his fear intensifies; Tolstoy begins to feel that nature, too, is synonymous with death. And so he tries increasingly to turn away from nature to God.

Tolstoy's horrified fixation with death, rooted in sensuous love of nature, leads him to a paradoxical reaction: it heightens his Rousseauism and perverts it. He retains all the Rousseauian hatred of civilization, but he endeavors to suppress the love of nature. Indeed, suppressing his love of nature makes his hatred of civilization more virulent. This dynamic, Mann says, has inscribed its dire signature on *Anna Karenina*, and one can see the short steps from it to "black reaction and barbarism" (1939, 187). In examining Tolstoy's pedagogical writings (written a decade before *Anna Karenina*) Mann finds the anger of primitive Russia against the liberalizing, European epoch; a hatred of humanistic civilization and an embracing of the nihilism and terrorism of the Bolshevik revolution. Levin's philosophy, Mann says, is a sign of the woeful direction the novelist was taking. "This Rousseauian quite sincerely considers all urban civilization, with the intellectual and cultural goings-on bound up in it, a sink of iniquity" (185). Levin's throwing over the scientific discipline of the nineteenth century and surrendering himself to "the 'mythus,' the 'faith'—in other words, to a paltry and culture-destroying vulgarity" (187) is a dangerous step in the direction of fascism. Mann says that Levin-Tolstoy forgets that the science of the nineteenth century—"all that the times teach him about organisms and their destruction, about the indestructibility of matter and the laws of conservation of energy, about evolution, and so forth" (187)—was directed by an impetus for the good. "He forgot that it was stern and bitter love of truth that made it [i.e., nineteenth-century thought] deny meaning to life. It too, denying God, lived for God. That, too, is possible, and Levin forgets it. Art he does not need even to forget; he knows, it seems, nothing about it, obviously thinking of it only as the society prattle of the 'cultured'" (188).

Tolstoy's radical asceticism, particularly evidenced in his pedagogical writings, in Levin's hostility toward culture and hatred of rationalism, looks ahead to the "romantic barbarism" (1922, 172) of the twentieth century, says Mann, rather than to the salvation of Tolstoy's soul.

Andre von Gronicka implies that Mann, in *The Magic Mountain* (1924), sought to celebrate the woman Tolstoy's pagan genius meant to create in *Anna Karenina*. The Russian Clavdia Chauchat, he says, insists on absolute personal freedom. Although married, she lives with a lover. She is contemptuous of the bourgeois conception of marriage with its underlying purpose of creating family and children. The passionate

Mynheer Peeperkorn, whom Clavdia loves, is based, von Gronicka (1947, 321) claims, on Tolstoy himself—Tolstoy, that is, the pagan sensualist who creates paeans to feeling and is terrified by death and loss of vitality. In Peeperkorn's last great dialogue with the prudent Hans Castorp, he breathes the fire that ought to have enveloped Anna. "Man is nothing but the organ through which God consummates his marriage with roused and intoxicated life. If man fails in feeling, it is blasphemy; it is the surrender of His masculinity, a cosmic catastrophe, an irreconcilable horror—' He drank" (Mann 1951, 603). But Tolstoy does not celebrate passion in *Anna Karenina*: having created it, he fights it.

Mann, like Lawrence, attacks Tolstoy for betraying his genius. What Lawrence calls "phallic splendour" Mann names "pagan sensuality," genius for life, a radiation of life. Mann, however, is on shaky ground when he explains Tolstoy's obsession with death and his hatred of civilization. He hints that his obsession is as much a Wagneresque romantic disease as a Christian-moral phenomenon. He seems, for his own purposes, to be turning Tolstoy into Wagner in order to exorcize the Wagner out of himself. Tolstoy-Wagner's tendency toward irrationalism and primitivism is to him an allegory of Germany's repudiating its faith in reason and the humanistic traditions of Western Europe for the mysticism and "romantic barbarism" of nazism. Mann, in short, is using Tolstoy as a stick to beat the Nazis.

Mann's attack on Levin must strike a responsive chord in many a reader. He says that *Anna Karenina* is artistically more satisfying than *War and Peace*. He even dubs it the "greatest society novel in all literature" (1939, 184). And yet he dislikes Levin and reads into the novel an odious tendency. The notion that *The Magic Mountain*, like some of Lawrence's work, was intended as a corrective to *Anna Karenina* is quite appealing. It was written at the same stage of Mann's development as his essay on Goethe and Tolstoy, and one can interpret the great polemical debate at the heart of Mann's novel to be between the healthy parliamentarian-humanist Goethe-Settembrini and the antirational West-hating Tolstoy-Naphta.

Georg Lukács

Georg Lukács, renowned for his writings on Marxist aesthetics, wrote a major essay on Tolstoy in 1936, which is reprinted in *Studies in European Realism* (1950). V. I. Lenin, says Lukács, was the only critic who provided the key to Tolstoy's greatness, regarding him as "the poet of the peasant revolt" (145). Tolstoy mirrored this epoch of widespread social unrest, which lasted from the abolition of serfdom in 1861 to the revolution of 1905, faithfully recording, "without his knowledge, and contrary to his conscious intentions" (137), the transformation of society caused by the growth of capitalism—an Asiatic form of capitalism, which tended to preserve the aristocracy and adapt it to the requirements of capitalistic interest. This interest, and the purpose of capitalism, which bureaucratized the Russian nobility, is "the protection, by any and every means, even the most brutal, of the private property owned by the ruling classes" (166).

Lukács contends that though the issues in *Anna Karenina* are presented "on an almost purely individual ethical basis: how can life be arranged in a way that men should not ruin themselves morally by exploiting the labour of others" and that though "Tolstoy has given plenty of incorrect and reactionary answers to this question," still there is "a paradoxical greatness in the fact that while his conscious striving was constantly directed toward the moral and religious overcoming of this rigid division of society into two hostile camps [i.e., landowners and peasants], . . . the reality which he depicted with relentless fidelity constantly exposed the impracticability of this the author's favourite dream" (146–47).

What matters, says Lukács, is not whether the content of Tolstoy's gospel is true or false. Tolstoy preaches plenty of "reactionary nonsense . . . what matters is the social movement of which this gospel, for all the falseness of its content, was yet the ideological expression" (194). Moreover, he says, "nothing could be cheaper and more vulgar than to regard these strivings of Tolstoy merely from the angle of the imperfection of his thinking . . . as so many 'practical' Western critics of Tolstoy have done" (256). To Lukács, the "liberals" and "progressives" who sneer at Tolstoy as a reactionary fail to see in *Anna Karenina* a subtle and masterful exposé of the evils of capitalism.

Lukács says that V. I. Lenin "demonstrated most convincingly that when Tolstoy so aptly and so venomously criticized the Russian society of his time, he did so almost entirely from the viewpoint of a naive 'patriarchal' peasant" (127). This, Lukács submits, is the Tolstoyan angle of vision in *Anna Karenina*. Tolstoy's principal characters exist "as a function of their connection with the exploitation of the peasantry" and their lives depend on their social position as parasites (176–77). The effect of capitalization and bureaucratization on the ruling classes is portrayed with extraordinary clarity. Tolstoy sees how the exploiters themselves are not only transformed into "mere malignant robots . . . but also how this whole process turns against these same human beings at every point in their lives, whenever they attempt to defend their own elementary vital interests or manifest a remnant of humanity still surviving within themselves" (163). Karenin is the most extreme illustration of the dehumanizing process. "Not until he stands beside Anna's sick-bed and her profound suffering affects him with physical directness, are the rigid, mechanized, automatically functioning elements of his personality loosened to some extent; in his deeply buried human core something like real life begins to stir. But as this stirring is much too weak to establish new human relations between him and Anna, he soon sinks back into an increased rigidity; the 'human' traits of his later days are mere hypocrisy, a mere religious mask on the face of this internally petrified bureaucrat" (188). Lukács describes Karenin as do most Western critics. But he interprets Karenin's failure to love not as something rooted in the psyche of the individual man but as something imposed on him by the "lies, hypocrisy and dehumanization, which are brought about by capitalism" (166).

Even Vronsky, whose energies are liberated by love, cannot escape the constricting influences of capitalism. "When he returns to Russia the inverse process begins at once: his reconversion into a pleasant average aristocrat with perfect manners in whom a great passion is something 'eccentric' and not organically linked with the central interests of his life. The conventional hardening that results does not go so far in Vronski as in Karenin, but it is sufficient to lead inevitably to Anna's tragic catastrophe" (188).

In this society of inhuman competition and exploitation, the few people capable of genuine feeling are doomed to perish. Lukács devotes very little space to Anna, but he manages to voice two contradictory perspectives on her function in the novel. She is crushed by the callousness and hypocrisy of her husband and society and by the growing coldness of her lover—that is, by the social forces unleashed by the growth of capitalism in postemancipation Russia. From this perspective, she is the accuser of bourgeois-capitalistic society. But Lukács also refers to her as "a blindly infatuated society lady" (193) and says that this perspective on her follows from Tolstoy's "acceptance of the peasant point of view" (193). On the one hand, Anna is a victim of capitalism; on the other hand, since the novel's real angle of vision is the perspective of the exploited peasant, she is one of the exploiters and her suffering is inconsequential. Indeed, the overriding interest of the Marxist critic is in the Levin-Tolstoy plot, since the novel is a historical document of peasant unrest, capitalism's evils, and reactionary landowner ideology during the period when Russia is headed toward its revolution. Can there be real tragedy in the love of a highborn lady in this exploitative and decadent society beginning to prepare itself for the majestic event? Lukács says that "the fact that this form of tragedy has its origin in an idle parasitic life is always kept before our eyes" (193).

Levin, of course, is another matter. He too is one of Tolstoy's superb types of the Russian nobility undergoing bureaucratization and dehumanization, but while he is an exploitative landowner fighting to recover his material prosperity, he tries at the same time not to fall victim to the capitalization of the land. Furthermore, he cannot convince himself that his existence as a landowner is justified and that he has a right to exploit his peasants. Sometimes he "leans towards a straightforward reactionary conservatism, while at other times he finds the arguments against private ownership of the land irrefutable" (186). His role as exploiter is ever-present in his thoughts as an "'extreme possibility' of a permanent crisis" (183), and his "zigzag path" (186) represents yet another phenomenon of a doomed nobility in a Russia that has been turned upside down on the eve of the Revolution.

Lukács's discussion tends to turn the novel into a stilted allegory. Everything is seen as a poetic reflection of V. I. Lenin's conception of Russia's postemancipation, prerevolutionary period; Lenin's is "the only correct view" (128). The novel, according to this point of view, has no universality, or rather, the only issue of universal importance is the human struggle against the deforming influences of capitalism. This is the given. Since to Lukács the novel's angle of vision is that of the exploited peasant, what is there to say of Anna that can conceivably be of interest? The Soviet critic Bychkov is more interested in Anna's tragedy as a real tragedy. But he strips from the novel all idea of Anna's interior life as being legitimately part of Tolstoy's portrayal of the woman, because to him she is an illustration of what capitalism does to people who have the capacity for genuine feeling. Lukács refers to Anna in both ways—as the subject of a trivial, personal tragedy and as an illustration of the greater tragedy of capitalism: "What is outside the average in Anna Karenina's figure and fate is not some individually pathological exaggeration of a personal passion. . . . When Anna Karenina breaks through the limits of the commonplace, she merely brings to the surface in tragically clear intensification the contradications latently present . . . in every *bourgeois* love and marriage" (176). And nothing else about one of the most rich and enigmatic characters in literature! Incidentally, Lukács, with his narrow doctrines, righteous notions, and hostility against the West is the model for Thomas Mann's reactionary Jesuit, Naphta, in *The Magic Mountain*.

Edward Wasiolek

Boris Eikhenbaum calls Anna's fate the judgment of her avenging conscience; her "own moral court" turns her passion into "tedium, hate, jealousy . . . into a 'fateful duel'" (*Seventies*, 145–46). Wasiolek contends that Anna is destroyed, not by conscience or God, but by the nature of sexual passion itself. He says that Tolstoy's characters come close to a genuine, inner core of experience when they act spontaneously and intensely in relation to nature or other people, but that this "'right' experience" (1978, 5) is perverted by sexual passion as well as institutionalized codes of behavior. In *Anna Karenina* the life-force of healthy egocentricism, by which characters come into contact with this precious center, assumes the dark outline of sexual passion, becoming a destructive force. Thus Anna's destructive behavior proceeds from the very nature of sex; Tolstoy takes "this beautiful and life-loving woman from plenitude and happiness to barrenness and destruction because of his own distorted sexual views and his own inadequate conception of love and sex" (10).

Wasiolek also explains Anna's motives in terms of Freudian psychology. The novel is a psychoanalytic drama in which Karenin and Vronsky are paternal figures, and Anna reenacts the anguish of a child who is abandoned by her father "because of the intervening and hateful mother" (157). Wasiolek's psychoanalytic thesis addresses Matthew Arnold's and Percy Lubbock's astonishment that such an extraordinary woman should fall in love with an ordinary cavalry officer. Yet her passion is understandable when one realizes that Vronsky has fundamental similarities to her husband and she has a deep-seated need to feel rejected. He is ambitious like Karenin, and a social creature through and through. Indeed, Anna chooses him because of these traits. He is generous and chivalrous, but callous, with a tenacity that will bear well the total absorption of her love.

Anna comes to Moscow on a mission of "domestic counseling," a woman "wisely past the turbulence of life" (133). The "hidden Anna" makes her first appearance at the ball, "the Anna of suppressed hunger for passion" (133). The scene on the train celebrates the emergence of a new woman in her. She falls for Vronsky because the "new Anna" needs a lover with whom to keep her love unsatisfied.

Her affair with Vronsky is a succession of provoked complications, from the arranged accident in 4:2, when, throwing caution to the winds, she summons him to her home and he runs into her husband, to their final quarrel. Every step of the way, she rejects what might be solutions to her terrible situation in order "to keep the tie tight . . . even if it must be done by punishment, guilt, and self-destruction" (143). Wasiolek's eye is on both his readings. Either Tolstoy sees this behavior to be in the nature of sexual passion, or he has caught the drama of the terrified child.

Divorce from Karenin, says Wasiolek, was never a real issue for Anna. When Karenin offers it, along with custody of her son, she refuses, and her excuse that she will not take advantage of his magnanimity is not believable. Having made her brutally honest declaration to him after the races, she never takes his feelings into account. Could she have been as passionately happy in Italy if Seryozha were there? Wasiolek says that the loss of her son and social ostracism are secondary issues; what she is terrified of is losing Vronsky. She courts humiliation by attending the opera, wanting the isolation from society in order to possess him more completely.

Wasiolek says that "Tolstoy sees sex as a massive intrusion on a person's being and a ruthless obliteration of the sanctity of personhood"

(154) and that sex and death are entwined, sex serving death "almost in eerie anticipation of the Marcusian interpretation of Freud, in which the sexual impulse is seen to be in the service of the death instinct" (162). In short, sex, in the case of Anna Karenina, is a disease.

> In the early works, including *War and Peace*, the sex is highly subli-mated; the relations between men and women are childlike. They are either official and matrimonial, or they are pure and ideal. . . . There is awe, pity, and sympathy, but no quickening of the veins. There are, to be sure, Princess Ellen and Anatole Kuragin, and dark sexual crimes are hinted about them, but that is precisely the point: sexuality is a dark sexual crime and Princess Ellen is a "dirty" woman. . . . We have to confront the fact that Tolstoy was a genius who had an unhealthy view of sex. (9–10)

Wasiolek psychoanalyzes the author and the character separately. Looking at Tolstoy's motives he says that Anna is destroyed because she is contaminated by sex, whereas Kitty and Levin's union is clean. Focus-ing on the character's motives he says, "Anna courts abandonment by in-sulting Vronsky and pushing him to hate her" (156). She needs to feel "hateful and corrupt" and has an obsessive need to feel he loves someone else. These destructive drives are so deep and powerful that they have originated in childhood, and he theorizes (for nothing is told of Anna's childhood) that some psychic need was being satisfied when she chose to marry into an emotionless relationship with Karenin. "This hypothesis takes on some credence when we see that Vronsky, for whom Anna abandons Karenin, in many ways resembles her husband. From Vronsky too Anna suffers from the threat of abandonment, and from a coldness that she discerns in him and projects onto him" (156–57).

The crux of this reading is that Anna neurotically picks in Vronsky "someone who will hurt her" (157) just as her husband (and her father) had hurt her. In the twilight hours before her suicide, according to Wasiolek, Anna behaves like a child, waiting for Vronsky to tuck her in, kissing her own hand as a mother kisses a hurt child, and remembering her childhood before throwing herself under the train. In Wasiolek's Freudian diagram, Vronsky's mother becomes the other woman for whom Vronsky is betraying her. "It takes only the mildest of displacements to shift the cause of being unloved and abandoned by Vronsky from Vronsky's mother to her own mother. And if Vronsky represents for Anna's psyche a repetition of Karenin and the paternal image, then Anna in her last delusional hours reenacts a drama of terrified child facing abandonment by the father because of the intervening and hateful mother" (157).

This is stimulating criticism. It gives the novel a twist of the screw, exaggerating things, which can be an effective way of looking at them, as if through a microscope. Wasiolek's view that Anna is driven to death by Tolstoy's psychological disgust for sex is allied with my own view that Tolstoy suffers from moralistic disgust. Wasiolek's thesis revolves on a perception of Vronsky. Matthew Arnold and Percy Lubbock were perplexed by Anna's choice and her reckless abandon. Wasiolek says she's demonic because that's the way Tolstoy perceives passion and that she falls for the very man who will both disappoint her and endure her powerful emotional demands. She relentlessly woos and provokes him for demonstrations of passion; finally, she kills herself to set flowing, not his tenderness, but something closely akin to it—grief-stricken remorse.

In the grips of this derangement, Anna perceives social respectability and custody of her son as impediments to her love. Nothing matters but the tie with Vronsky. She squeezes dry the springs of his passion until she kills herself to draw from him the final drops.

This is indeed putting Anna under the microscope, and perhaps the enlargement is too fantastic. In Wasiolek's view, the novel contrasts two kinds of love (Anna's and Levin's), but although Tolstoy regards one as dirty and the other as clean, in fact both are unhealthy.

Final Observation

All of these versions of Tolstoy are illuminating: Lawrence's pagan celebrator of sensuous life and sexual love whose novel is about social oppression and failed liberation; Mann's violent antihumanist, whose antagonism to nineteenth-century thought and all things European looks toward Stalin and Hitler; Lukács's poet of the postemancipation, whose depiction of agrarian problems and the rise of capitalism forecasts the coming of the Revolution; and Wasiolek's psychodramatist whose fear of supplanting the idealized image of his mother leads to distorted sexual attitudes. One final view of the novel seems important. This is Richard Gustafson's (1986) version of Tolstoy as a theologian in the Eastern Christian tradition, who teaches his religious worldview through extended parables about two ways of living—for oneself or for others.

Writing in the style of exegetical scholarship, Gustafson says that to understand Tolstoy, one must look at his writings as a whole. Each of his texts takes its meaning from the oeuvre, and "[t]he primary rule in reading Tolstoy, therefore, is that the later clarifies the earlier" (7). Tolstoy's life work consists of experiments in different genres, all of which tell religious stories in which character, setting, and plot embody spiritual values and portray two ways of being in the world—a moral vision that, in *Anna*

Karenina, is symbolized by the painting of Pilate and Christ. Anna remains the self-absorbed personality wishing the greatest possible fullness of life for herself, whereas Levin becomes a true Christian who discovers his divine self. Anna makes the mistake of living for romance, failing to perceive that "the mission" for which human beings are sent to earth is to do good for others. Doing good merges the striving self with the unity of everything "hidden from us by time," when people were "animals, trees, flowers, the earth" (9). Fear of death recedes when one is doing good for its own sake; Levin learns that his reward is fearlessness in the face of death and a return to the primary unity in all creation.

Gustafson points to Dostoyevsky's Father Zossima as the icon of an orthodoxy to which Tolstoy and others belong. To Zossima, the earth is God's garden in which human growth depends on contact with the supernatural; this heavenly contact is maintained through love of all God's creation. Zossima's "active love" is God's love in man, given to be expressed; only divine love frees one from isolation, bitterness, and death. Anna, in other words, should have found in marriage not her punishment, but her purpose. "The tragedy of the watchman who does not watch," who is crushed by the train and returns to haunt her dreams, "is the emblem of that suppression of conscience which results in death" (120). Anna cannot face her conscience any more than she can force her brother to own up to his misdeeds; she transfers her guilt to Karenin and Vronsky, making them responsible for her dilemma. "She trivializes Karenin's emotions and then turns them against him. He is the one who is guilty" (122). The more she suffers, the less she can forgive him. The steeplechase accident reveals to Vronsky his worst fears: "He has made a wrong movement, and his position is changed. He has spoiled his career, made Anna unhappy and pregnant, probably destroyed her honor and her life, and therefore his. Vronsky assumes total responsibility and accepts the displaced guilt. But the kick in the belly betrays his resentment" (124). Thus, by thrusting blame on others, Anna creates a dialectic of guilt and escalating resentment, and this shapes the pattern of her story. Her final moments express "the inevitable conclusion to be drawn from life understood as individual self-fulfillment" (130).

Levin, by contrast, corrects his flawed way of seeing, learning about love from suffering. Nikolai is an emblem of his mortality, and Nikolai's death scene, for Gustafson, is the heart of the novel. "In the face of death Kitty gives forth of herself. And this Levin learns. As the hour of death approaches, Nicholas asks Levin to sit with him. Nicholas extends his hand, and Levin grasps it. The 'question of death' recedes as Levin turns his attention to 'what he must do now, right now.' In giving forth of himself 'now, right now,' Levin has found his love" (139). Anna, by contrast, who has no faith, ends in suicide.

The problem with this otherwise astute reading is that it strips the great novel of ambiguity. It denies the fact that Anna takes the book away from Levin. Her story is an immense psychological account of a guilty soul's self-punishment—immense because of the fullness and concreteness with which Tolstoy dramatizes her contradictory impulses. She is never degraded, nor do her sufferings appear arbitrary, despite the anxiety, even torment Tolstoy endured in being artistically faithful to her. He evidently made good use of his anxiety. In his crisis of faith, with his whole nature bent on spiritual wrestling, and wishing with all his heart to make short shrift of Anna, he took excruciating pains to dramatize her suicidal course, evidently finding her anguish, as well as Levin's, within himself. The repentant and unrepentant sides of Tolstoy—these are the hero and heroine of his novel.

Notes

1. I do not mean to imply that Tolstoy experienced a solidity with authority or with some preexisting status quo. This was never true of Tolstoy, certainly not at the time of *Anna Karenina*.

2. Other interpretations of the moral vision, as well as a fuller presentation of Gustafson, appears in the last section "Perspectives on the Novel."

3. The quote is from a letter by I. Aksakov who is paraphrasing some of Wilhelm Riehl's ideas.

4. The quote is from the sixth edition of Riehl's book *Bourgeois Society* (1866).

5. Tolstoy found inspiration for his pedagogical career in Bertold Auerbach's *New Life* (1852), in which the hero, a nobleman, condemns half measures of sympathizing with the poor and being a communist in theory and advocates making a strong personal commitment. Auerbach's prince becomes a country teacher, and Tolstoy followed his example.

6. Educational theorists have discussed Tolstoy as an innovative thinker. Michael Armstrong says that Tolstoy regarded mental growth as "an unending effort to restore an inner harmony that is constantly threatened by development" (Pinch and Armstrong 1982, 63). Consequently, he was opposed to "the compulsory school with its characteristic discipline, and its standardised content, methods and assessments: a structure of meaning which it seeks to impose on all its pupils irrespective of circumstance" (31). He believed that "the person being educated must have the full power to express his dissatisfaction, or at least to withdraw from that part of education which does not satisfy his instinct, that there is only one criterion of pedagogy—freedom'" (33). Conversation was for Tolstoy the model of all educational relationships.

7. Tolstoy founded the school in 1859 and for the most part stopped teaching there himself in October 1862. It continued with hired teachers for years to come.

8. Tolstoy's original plan was for a vast epic about the Decembrist revolt of 1825. This he began researching in the summer of 1863.

9. These friends were M. P. Pogodin, S. S. Urov, Yu F. Samarin, and S. Urusov. Urusov facetiously defined Westernizers as follows: "Who, for example, are the people who are called *Westernizers* in Russia? Not those who shave their beards, not those who foster the development of the arts and sciences, not even those who patronize the Germans, love Western languages and attempt to develop the Russian people in an artificial coercive manner. Instead, the name Westernizer refers to those who, under the pretext of enlightenment, uproot our innate love of truth, simplicity, order, and justice and replace it with decadent Western moral principles" (Eikhenbaum *Sixties*, 211–12).

10. In 1886 his wife S. A. Tolstaya restored the philosophical discourses and created the familiar four-volume structure in the fifth edition of *War and Peace*.

11. In the passage from which I have drawn these quotations, Mann describes Tolstoy's love-hate relationship with Shakespeare. Tolstoy's attraction to the Greeks was similarly ambiguous.

12. Pinch and Armstrong discuss the *Primer* as an effort to create a transitional literature that would enable the common people to make the giant step from folk culture, that is, proverbs and riddles, to literary language and high culture. But the last thing Tolstoy wanted was for his peasants to become representatives of the high culture and skilled users of that literary language.

13. Troyat writes of the autobiographical features of Levin's portrait: "He shamelessly attributed to him the events of his own life, fed him with his ideas, the books he read, his own blood. The relationship between Levin and Kitty—the declaration scene using the first letters of words, the wedding ceremony, including the last-minute hesitation and the incident of the forgotten shirt in the trunk, the young couple's first days in their country home, the birth of their first child—were one and all transposed from the author's past. . . . Levin's relations with his muzhiks are drawn directly from Tolstoy's experience at Yasnaya Polyana" (1967, 363). However, as S. P. Bychkov notes, "[t]he closeness of the hero to the author is determined not by everyday details, which were based on life at Yasnaya Polyana, but by the extraordinary similarity in their ideological and religious pursuits" (1970, 823–24).

14. William James treats Tolstoy's melancholia and conversion at some length in his classic study *The Varieties of Religious Experience*. "When disillusionment has gone as far as this, there is seldom a *restitutio ad integrum*. One has tasted of the fruit of the tree, and the happiness of Eden never comes again. The happiness that comes, when any does come—and often enough it fails to return in an acute form, though its form is sometimes very acute—is not the simple ignorance of ill, but something vastly more complex, including natural evil as one of its elements, but finding natural evil no such stumblingblock and terror because it now sees it swallowed up in supernatural good. The process is one of redemption, not of mere reversion to natural health, and the sufferer, when

Notes

saved, is saved by what seems to him a second birth, a deeper kind of conscious being than he could enjoy before" (James 1985, 131).

15. At that time the Orthodox church was the state religion. Its theology was, in some respects, the nation's law. For example, the law on divorce was the church's law. It allowed only two grounds: incompetence (inability to consummate the marriage) and adultery. And, actually, the first was grounds for annulment rather than divorce. Thus, for divorce to take place, adultery had to be proved (or admitted). The guilty party was subsequently not allowed to remarry in the church and not allowed custody of any issue of the marriage.

16. Bloom 1981, 211–31.

Armstrong relies greatly on Jean Laplanche's *Life and Death and Psychoanalysis* (1976) in her discussion of Anna's narcissism and death drive. As already noted, Anna's narcissism originates in having been deprived of family life as a child. Wasiolek intensifies this idea in his analysis, saying that Anna's anxiety is generated by a childhood compulsion to act out, with both Vronsky and Karenin, the experience of being abandoned by her father.

17. This quotation from Freud's "The Most Prevalent Form of Degradation in Erotic Life," is part of Armstrong's analysis, which relies heavily on Denis de Rougement's standard work on love and death, *Passion and Society* (1962).

18. In the discussion of Lawrence's attitude toward *Anna Karenina* I am indebted to David J. Gordon. See Bibliography.

19. I have revised H. T. Lowe-Porter's translation of the final phrase to conform to the text printed in Thomas Mann, *Leiden und Grosse der Meister.* (Gesammelte Werke in Einzelbanden, Frankfurter Ausgabe), ed. Peter de Mendelssohn (Frankfurt: S. Fischer Verlag, 1982), p. 116: "denn Todesfurcht, diese Quelle von Tolstois Poesie und Religiositat, ist Natur-Liebesfrucht."

Works Cited

Primary

Anna Karenina. Translated by Constance Garnett. Edited and introduced by Leonard J. Kent and Nina Berberova. Modern Library College Editions. New York: Modern Library, 1965.

Confession. Translated with an introduction by David Patterson. New York and London: W. W. Norton & Co., 1983.

"Diary of a Madman." In *A First Series of Representative Russian Stories: Pushkin to Gorky*, selected and edited and with an introduction by Janko Lavrin. London: Westhouse, 1946.

Tolstoy's Diaries. Edited and translated by R. F. Christian. 2 vols. New York: Charles Scribner's Sons, 1985. Begun in January 1847, the diaries are a "lifelong witness of the dialogue between exacting spirit and rebellious flesh."

Tolstoy's Letters. Translated by R. F. Christian. 2 vols. New York: Charles Scribner's Sons, 1978.

War and Peace. The Maude Translation. Backgrounds and Sources; Essays in Criticism, edited by George Gibian. A Norton Critical Edition. New York and London: W. W. Norton & Co., 1966.

Secondary

Books

Armstrong, Judith M. *The Unsaid Anna Karenina*. New York: St. Martin's Press, 1988. A Freudian and feminist interpretation of the novel, with highly stimulating results.

Works Cited

Bayley, John. *Tolstoy and the Novel.* New York: Viking Press, 1966. One of the most important general studies of Tolstoy in English.

Berlin, Isaiah. *The Hedgehog and the Fox: An Essay on Tolstoy's View of History.* New York: Simon & Schuster, 1967. Originally published 1953. This philosophical treatise presents Tolstoy's historical theory as the key to his complex and divided personality.

Christian, R. F. *Tolstoy: A Critical Introduction.* Cambridge: At the University Press, 1969. One of the best critical introductions to Tolstoy in English. Like Bayley's book, it is well informed, scholarly, and lucidly and agreeably written. It is especially useful in its concern with Tolstoy's method of composition and the technique of his craft.

Eikhenbaum, Boris. *Tolstoy in the Sixties.* Translated by Duffield White. Ann Arbor, Mich.: Ardis, 1982.

_____. *Tolstoy in the Seventies.* Translated by Albert Kaspin. Ann Arbor, Mich.: Ardis, 1982. These studies by perhaps the greatest modern Russian literary historian (1886–1959) describe Tolstoy's contradictory responses to the social and cultural life of his time. *Tolstoy in the Sixties* also analyzes the varied and complex creative impulses that went into the writing of *War and Peace. Tolstoy in the Seventies* is an indispensable guide to the evolution of Tolstoy's thought during the genesis of *Anna Karenina.*

Gifford, Henry, ed. *Tolstoy: A Critical Anthology.* Harmondsworth, England: Penguin Books, 1971. This anthology spans more than one hundred years of Tolstoy criticism—from 1865 to 1969.

Gifford, Henry. *Tolstoy.* Past Masters Series. Oxford and New York: Oxford University Press, 1982.

Gorki, Maksim. *Reminiscences of Leo Nikolaevich Tolstoy.* Authorized translation from the Russian by S. S. Koteliansky and Leonard Woolf. New York: B. W. Huebsch, 1920. These fragmentary reminiscences are generally thought to be of the highest biographical importance. The book is ardent, candid, and beautifully written.

Gustafson, Richard F. *Leo Tolstoy, Resident and Stranger: A Study in Fiction and Theology.* Princeton: Princeton University Press, 1986. An impressive scholarly study of Tolstoy as a religious thinker.

Hardy, Thomas. *Tess of the d'Urbervilles.* Edited by Scott Elledge. Norton Critical Edition. New York and London: W. W. Norton, 1979.

James, William. *The Varieties of Religious Experience.* The Works of William James, edited by Frederick H. Burkhardt, Fredson Bowers, and Ignas K. Skrupskelis. Cambridge, Mass. and London: Harvard University Press, 1985. Originally published 1902.

Knowles, A. V., ed. *Tolstoy: The Critical Heritage.* The Critical Heritage Series. London, Henley, and Boston: Routledge & Kegan Paul, 1978. Knowles's introduction describes the literary scene during Tolstoy's creative life and outlines the critical reception to his writings. The volume consists of 121 passages selected from the vast amount of critical literature on Tolstoy written both inside and outside Russia from 1852 to 1910.

Lawrence, D. H. *Studies in Classic American Literature.* New York: Thomas Seltzer, 1923.

_____. *Phoenix: The Posthumous Papers of D. H. Lawrence.* Edited with an introduction by Edward D. McDonald. New York: Viking Press, 1936.

_____. *Psychoanalysis and the Unconscious and Fantasia of the Unconscious.* New York: Viking Press, 1960. First published 1921, 1922.

_____. *The Collected Letters of D. H. Lawrence.* Edited with an introduction by Harry T. Moore. 2 vols. New York: Viking Press, 1962.

_____. *Reflections on the Death of a Porcupine.* Bloomington: Indiana University Press, 1963. First Published 1925.

Leavis, F. R. *Anna Karenina and Other Essays.* New York: Pantheon Books, 1967. First published 1933.

Lubbock, Percy. *The Craft of Fiction.* London: Jonathan Cape, 1921.

Lukács, George. *Studies in European Realism: A Sociological Survey of the Writings of Balzac, Stendahl, Zola, Tolstoy, Gorki, and Others.* Translated by Edith Bone. London: Hillway Publishing Co., 1950. One of the master critics of our century; Lukács's chapters on Tolstoy are indispensable to readers interested in Marxist theory.

Mann, Thomas. *The Magic Mountain.* Translated by H. T. Lowe-Porter. New York: Alfred A. Knopf, 1951. First published 1924.

Maude, Aylmer. *The Life of Tolstoy.* 2 vols. London: Oxford University Press, 1930. Originally published (in a different form) 1908. Maude was an intimate of Tolstoy, and the two-volume study was completed during Tolstoy's life and corrected by his wife. The work is a useful reference for moderating the often savagely caustic biography by Troyat.

Merejkowski, Dmitri. *Tolstoy as Man and Artist, with an Essay on Dostoievski.* Westminster: Archibald Constable & Co., 1902. Without a doubt one of the most influential studies of Tolstoy.

Mirsky, D. S. *A History of Russian Literature from its Beginnings to 1900.* New York: Vintage Books, 1958. This literary history is a point of reference for all subsequent scholarly studies.

Nabokov, Vladimir. *Lectures on Russian Literature.* Edited with an introduction by Fredson Bowers. New York: Harcourt Brace Jovanovich, 1981. Lectures derived from notes Nabokov made for his literature classes at Wellesley and Cornell from 1941 to 1958. The best of them is on Tolstoy and is highly recommended.

Nehls, Edward, ed. *D. H. Lawrence: A Composite Biography.* 3 vols. Madison: University of Wisconsin Press, 1957, 1958, 1959.

Works Cited

Noyes, George Rapall. *Tolstoy.* Master Spirits of Literature. New York: Duffield & Co., 1918. This early study is useful for Rousseau's influence on Tolstoy.

Pinch, Alan, and Armstrong, Michael, ed. *Tolstoy on Education: Tolstoy's Educational Writings.* Teaneck, N.J.: Fairleigh Dickinson University Press, 1982. A study of Tolstoy as an educational theorist, with a collection of his pedagogical writings.

Schultze, Sydney. *The Structure of Anna Karenina.* Ann Arbor, Mich.: Ardis, 1982. A study of imagery, symbolism, themes, and character development.

Simmons, Ernest J. *Introduction to Tolstoy's Writings.* Chicago and London: University of Chicago Press, Phoenix Books, 1968. A very convenient quick reference for the story lines and main details of Tolstoy's work.

Steiner, George. *Tolstoy or Dostoevsky: An Essay in the Old Criticism.* New York: Alfred A. Knopf, 1959. Erudite, energetic, lucid, at times ardent, this book is a classic in the genre of literary criticism. Steiner is most brilliant in his discussion of Tolstoy as an epic poet.

Stenbock-Fermor, Elizabeth. *The Architecture of Anna Karenina: A History of Its Writing, Structure, and Message.* Lisse: The Peter de Ridder Press, 1975. This is a useful guide to the novel's structure.

Thorlby, Anthony. *Tolstoy: Anna Karenina.* Landmarks of World Literature. Cambridge: At the University Press, 1987. A highly intelligent, movingly written study of the novel.

Tolstoy, Sophia. *The Diaries of Sophia Tolstoy.* Translated by Cathy Porter. New York: Random House, 1985. Unfortunately the selection is rather too spotty.

Troyat, Henri. *Tolstoy.* Translated by Nancy Amphoux. Garden City, N.Y.: Doubleday & Co., 1967. Written with a novelist's skill, this is a moving and often caustic account of Tolstoy's life, dealing fully, and perhaps too inventively, with the external details of daily life and the intimate relations of husband and wife.

Turgenev, Ivan. *Turgenev's Letters.* Selected, translated, and edited by A. V. Knowles. London: Athlone Press, 1983.

Walicki, Andrzej. *The Slavophile Controversy: History of a Conservative Utopia in Nineteenth-Century Russian Thought.* Translated by Hilda Andrews-Rusiecka. Oxford: Clarendon Press, 1975. Originally published in Polish in 1964. Regarded as a major contribution to the study of nineteenth-century thought, this is a lucid and well-written account of a world of ideas totally opposed to contemporary socialist, Utopian, and Marxist thought.

Wasiolek, Edward. *Tolstoy's Major Fiction.* Chicago and London: University of Chicago Press, 1978. Always interesting, his chapter on *Anna Karenina* offers a psychoanalytic reading that is daring and fresh. Highly recommended.

Wilson, A. N. *Tolstoy.* New York: W. W. Norton, 1988. A wonderful new biography and an excellent starting point for students of Tolstoy.

Woolf, Virginia. *The Common Reader.* 1925. Reprint. New York: Harcourt, Brace & World, 1953.

Articles and Parts of Books

Arnold, Matthew. "Count Leo Tolstoi." In *Essays in Criticism: Second Series.* London: Macmillan & Co., 1888.

Blackmur, R. P. "The Dialectic of Incarnation." In *Tolstoy: A Collection of Critical Essays,* edited by Ralph E. Matlaw. Twentieth Century Views. Englewood Cliffs, N.J.: Prentice-Hall, 1967. First published 1950. An influential essay.

Bloom, Harold. "Freud and the Poetic Sublime." In *Freud: A Collection of Critical Essays,* edited by Perry Meisel. Englewood Cliffs: Prentice-Hall, 1981.

Bychkov, S. P. "The Social Bases of Anna Karenina." In Leo Tolstoy, *Anna Karenina.* The Maude Translation. Backgrounds and Sources; Essays in Criticism. Edited by George Gibian. A Norton Critical Edition. New York and London: W. W. Norton & Co., 1970. First published 1965.

Cook, Albert, "The Moral Vision: Tolstoy." In *Tolstoy: A Collection of Critical Essays,* edited by Ralph E. Matlaw. Twentieth Century Views. Englewood Cliffs, N.J.: Prentice-Hall, 1967. First published 1960.

Hardy, Thomas. "Candor in English Fiction." In *Thomas Hardy's Personal Writings,* edited by Harold Orel. Lawrence: University of Kansas Press, 1966.

Jahn, Gary R. "The Image of the Railroad in Anna Karenina." *Slavic and East European Journal* 25, no. 2 (Summer 1981): 1–10.

————. "Tolstoi, Lev Nikolaevich." In *Handbook of Russian Literature,* edited by Victor Terras. New Haven and London: Yale University Press, 1985. Jahn provides a useful outline of Tolstoy's life and works. The reader might see as well Wasiolek's and Christian's chronologies.

Kurrik, Maire Jaanus. "Tolstoy's *Anna Karenina*: The Self's Negativity." In *Leo Tolstoy's Anna Karenina,* edited by Harold Bloom. New York: Chelsea House, 1987.

Lenin, V. I. "Leo Tolstoy as the Mirror of the Russian Revolution." In *Collected Works,* vol. 15, edited by Andrew Rothstein and Bernard Isaacs. Moscow: Foreign Languages Publishing House, 1963. The essay was originally published in 1908.

————. "Lev Tolstoi and His Epoch." In *Collected Works,* vol. 17, edited by George Hanna. Moscow: Foreign Languages Publishing House, 1963. The essay was originally published in 1911. Lukács and all Marxist critics have done endless obeisances to Lenin's numerous essays on Tolstoy, especially those cited here.

Mann, Thomas. "Anna Karenina." In *Essays of Three Decades,* translated by H. T. Lowe-Porter. New York: Alfred A. Knopf, 1947. First published 1939.

_____. "Goethe and Tolstoi." In *Essays of Three Decades,* translated by H. T. Lowe-Porter. New York: Alfred A. Knopf, 1947. First published 1922.

_____. "Goethe and Tolstoi." In *Leiden und Grosse der Meister.* Gesammelte Werke in Einzelbanden, Frankfurter Ausgabe, edited by Peter de Mendelssohn. Frankfurt: S. Fischer Verlag, 1982. First published 1922.

_____. "Tolstoi (On the Hundredth Anniversary of His Birth)." In *Past Masters and Other Papers,* translated by H. T. Lowe-Porter. Essay Index Reprint Series. Freeport, N.Y.: Books for Libraries Press, 1968. First published 1928.

Van Gronicka, Andre. "Thomas Mann and Russia." In *The Stature of Thomas Mann,* edited by Charles Neider. New York: New Directions, 1947. First published 1945.

Bibliography

Crankshaw, Edward. *Tolstoy: The Making of a Novelist.* New York: Viking, 1974. An extremely polished and caustic biography.

Gordon, David J. *D. H. Lawrence As a Literary Critic.* New Haven and London: Yale University Press, 1966. Contains the most useful summary of Lawrence's scattered remarks on Tolstoy.

Jahn, Gary R. "The Unity of Anna Karenina." *The Russian Quarterly Review* 41, no. 2 (April 1982): 144–58.

Matlaw, Ralph E., ed. *Tolstoy: A Collection of Critical Essays.* Twentieth Century Views. Englewood Cliffs, N.J.: Prentice-Hall, 1967.

Index

Index

The Author

Gary Adelman has been teaching English and European literature for twenty-five years at the University of Illinois at Urbana-Champaign. He has written scholarly articles, a novel, and poems and is the author of the Twayne study on Joseph Conrad's *Heart of Darkness* and a forthcoming study on Thomas Hardy's *Jude the Obscure.*